A Companion Text for *Kindred*

Fluency through Novels

A Companion Text
for *Kindred*

Janet Giannotti

Ann Arbor

THE UNIVERSITY OF MICHIGAN PRESS

Copyright © by the University of Michigan 1999
All rights reserved
ISBN 978-0-472-08552-1
Published in the United States of America by
The University of Michigan Press
Printed and bound by CPI Group (UK) Ltd, Croydon, CR0 4YY

2015 2014 2013 2012   7 6 5 4

To Mollie and Matthew

Contents

To the Teacher

Introduction

Bookmarks: Fluency through Novels has been designed to help you and your students enjoy reading, discussing, and writing about novels. The purpose of the text is threefold. First, it can make a student's experience with a novel more successful and richer. Second, it cuts teacher preparation time and time spent in front of a copy machine. And third, the activities in Bookmarks address your students' multiple intelligences and give them choices in their learning.

Pacing

This volume of Bookmarks accompanies *Kindred* by Octavia Butler (the Beacon Press edition). The text divides the novel's 264 pages into six more-or-less equal sections plus a short Before You Begin section. The material in the text represents anywhere from 30 to 60 hours of instruction and can be covered in 6 weeks, 12 weeks, or a 14- to 16-week semester.

Before You Begin

Before students begin to read the novel on their own, work through the Before You Begin section with them. It's best to advise students to skip the "Introduction," as it is quite difficult and gives away a lot of the plot. Before You Begin covers pages 9 to 15 in the novel. Students may read these pages at home or in class, or you can read the section aloud to the class. After students have understood these pages, the Before You Begin section encourages freewriting and discussion of the concept of time travel and then introduces students to summarizing, response journals, and a vocabulary log.

Unit Format

Each of the six units in the text follows the same format. Students build fluency in reading, speaking, and writing as they complete a variety of exercises and activities that combine traditional methods with whole-language techniques.

Looking Ahead gives a short preview of the section of the novel that the unit covers. Note that each unit covers an average of 45 pages in the novel and that text units do not always correspond to chapters in the novel.

Freewriting asks students to freewrite for 15 minutes on a topic related to the section and should generally be done before students read the section. They may write about the novel or about their lives. Freewriting may be done in class or for homework, in a journal or on separate sheets of paper. It may be shared with the teacher or kept private. Each unit gives several freewriting topics so that students may have a choice of what to write on.

Test Yourself sections present several short quizzes of varying styles to test students' understanding of the plot. Note that quizzes often cover shorter segments of the novel; you may want to refer to the page numbers on the quizzes when giving daily reading assignments.

The quizzes in the Test Yourself sections serve not only to check comprehension but as an aid in comprehension. Note instructions for students to mark the sections of the novel where they find the answer and to share answers with their group. Students who find the novel difficult should participate in group discussion of the quizzes and then be encouraged to reread all or part of the section of the novel. Answers to all quizzes are provided in the Answer Key.

Vocabulary sections begin with instructions to add 10 words to a personal vocabulary log, which is introduced in Before You Begin. You may customize this section to suit your style and require words on cards or in a notebook. You may suggest words for your students to add to their lists, have the class select words as a group, or allow individuals to select their own words. You may test students on their lists or simply check to see that their lists are accurate and complete.

One or two vocabulary exercises also appear in the Vocabulary section. These help students practice choosing correct definitions in context, provide explanations for some terms, and give practice in finding and using other forms of words that appear in the novel. Answers to these vocabulary exercises are in the Answer Key.

Vocabulary exercises can be done at any time in the unit and do not necessarily need to be done after the quizzes and before Summarizing.

Summarizing sections contain one or more exercises to help students learn the skill of summarizing fiction and end with an assignment to summarize a short section of the novel. Summarizing is introduced in Before You Begin. This section can be done any time after students have completed the comprehension quizzes.

Response Journals are introduced in Before You Begin and are a good way for you to judge how well your students are connecting with the novel. The sections in each unit begin with an exercise that helps students respond to the novel. Exercises in the first three units help students see the difference between a response and a summary. In the last three units, students give short responses to several passages. Students may work in pairs or groups on these exercises. Each Response Journal section ends with an assignment to write two response journals. These may be kept in a spiral notebook or on separate sheets and should be checked to see if students have significant questions about or misunderstandings of the novel.

Topics for Discussion sections provide one or more topics that can be discussed in small groups or with the whole class. Often students are asked to put ideas into graphic organizers such as mind maps (webs) or Venn diagrams. Topics for Discussion can be done at any point in the unit but should be completed before students do the Composition section.

Composition provides an opportunity for more formal writing, often on one of the topics in the discussion section. Students are instructed to write papers, which can be interpreted as paragraphs or short essays or something in between. This section also introduces point-of-view writing and asks students to write letters from the point of view of various characters. Compositions can be done in class or for homework and can be reviewed, revised, and edited if you choose.

Beyond the Novel introduces historical, geographical, and cultural background to the novel. In each section some material is presented, usually in text form, and is followed by one or more exercises. Beyond the Novel sections can be covered out of order.

Options offers optional activities including puzzles and suggestions for role plays and library research.

Additional Sections

The final two sections of the book are Projects and the Answer Key.

Projects offers a list of ideas for projects that can be done during or after the reading of the novel. Projects can be presented throughout the semester or on one or two days after students have come to the end of the novel.

The Answer Key provides answers to many of the quizzes and exercises in the text.

Multiple Intelligences

Bookmarks asks students to do a wide variety of exercises and activities rather than repeating the same exercises in every unit. In this way, it is hoped that Bookmarks addresses the multiple intelligences of your students. Here are the ways in which Bookmarks addresses multiple intelligences.

- Students with strong *linguistic intelligence* probably already read well and will become leaders in group discussions about the quizzes. They will enjoy the vocabulary exercises, freewriting, journals, and compositions, as well as the puzzles in the Options sections.

- For students with strong *logical-mathematical intelligence*, Bookmarks offers sequencing exercises, time lines and work with dates, and Venn diagrams.

- Students with strong *kinesthetic intelligence* will enjoy moving around the room to work with different groups and will be most interested in dressing as a character, cooking food mentioned in the novel, or standing up to act out role plays.

- For students with strong *spatial intelligence*, Bookmarks presents maps and photographs and asks students to work with graphic organizers. Videos are suggested as supplements.

- Students with strong *musical intelligence* will be interested in the song "Follow the Drinking Gourd" and should be encouraged to choose a project that uses music.

- Those with strong *interpersonal intelligence* will appreciate the group discussion topics, role plays, and projects that can be done in groups.

- And finally, Bookmarks offers journals, individual vocabulary work, library research, and many choices to students with strong *intrapersonal intelligence.*

Bookmarks has been designed to help students understand and enjoy novels and to increase their fluency while they do so. If you keep in mind that students' early experiences with novels should be fun, and approach the exercises and activities in Bookmarks accordingly, then you are about to begin a very positive experience!

Enjoy!

To the Student

Congratulations! You are about to start one of the most rewarding projects of your ESL studies: a novel!

Before you get started, you might have a few questions.

Why should I read a novel?
Novels are actually easier to understand than some shorter pieces. Once you get used to the writer's style and vocabulary choice, and once you understand the basic plot of the story, the book seems easier and easier to read. So if it seems a little difficult at first, just stick with it.

Why should I read Kindred?
Kindred is a great novel for two reasons. First, it's a fascinating story. As soon as you start reading, you'll want to find out what happens next. Second, it teaches you a little about history in a very easy-to-understand way.

How can Bookmarks help me with the novel?
Bookmarks gives you simple quizzes to make sure you understand the novel and provides you with topics that you can talk and write about. It also helps you learn vocabulary and teaches you a little about the history, geography, and culture of the United States.

What do I have to do?
You have to do your best to keep up with the reading as your teacher assigns it. If your teacher assigns too much in one night, please speak up. Also, if there is something that you don't understand even after you take the quiz and reread, don't be afraid to ask your teacher or to write about your doubts in your response journal or freewriting.

What do I need before I begin?
You'll need a good dictionary and any other supplies that your teacher assigns, such as spiral notebooks or index cards.

Is that all?
That's all for now. The Before You Begin section in this text will tell you everything else you need to know to get started!

Enjoy!

Before You Begin

Please read pages 9 to 15 in *Kindred* before you do this section. Stop at the end of the paragraph that begins "I nodded."

Freewriting

Choose one of the following. Copy it and continue writing for about 10 minutes. Discuss your ideas with your classmates after you finish writing.

I think Dana was dreaming because . . .

I think Dana really traveled to a river because . . .

Summarizing

In order to enjoy *Kindred* (or any science fiction), you have to "suspend disbelief." That means that you have to believe that Dana truly vanishes from Kevin's presence and appears next to a river on page 13.

A good technique for keeping up with events in a novel, such as Dana's mysterious travel, is to write summaries of chapters or smaller sections. Throughout your reading of *Kindred*, you will be asked to summarize short sections. Summarizing is a skill that takes practice to master. You may have these questions about summarizing.

How long should my summary be in relation to the original?

How many details should I include?

What verb tense should I use?

Try these exercises to help answer the questions about how to write a summary.

Exercise 1. Below are four summaries of the same section of the novel. The section begins in the middle of page 13 on line 17 and ends on page 14 on line 33. Fill in the missing words in these summaries and discuss your answers with your classmates.

Summary 1: 10 words

Dana rescued _____ from a river, where he was _____.

Summary 2: 18 words

Dana found herself next to a _____. She noticed a

_____ drowning in the river. She rescued _____.

Summary 3: 61 words

Dana found herself next to a _____. She _____ a boy

in the river. He was _____. She _____ to him and

pulled him out of the _____. She used mouth-to-mouth

resuscitation to save the _____. The boy's _____

took him from Dana. The boy's father came and aimed a

_____ at Dana. Dana became _____ and returned

home.

Summary 4: 147 words

When _____ recovered from her dizziness, she found herself

next to a wide _____. She noticed a _____ in the

river. He was _____! She waded, then swam into the river

and pulled him _____. The boy's mother _____ him from

Dana, but Dana snatched him back. She used mouth-to-mouth

resuscitation to save the _____. After a moment, the

_____ accused Dana of killing the boy. Dana told her that she was _____ him and continued the mouth-to-mouth resuscita-

tion. After the boy started to breathe on his own, the mother grabbed

him. She called him "_____," and Dana thought that was quite

a _____ name. The boy clung to his mother, screaming loudly.

Then the boy's _____ came and aimed a _____ at Dana.

When she _____ the click of the rifle, she became _____

and everyone vanished; she was home again.

Exercise 2. Choose the summary that you liked the best and compare your choice with your classmates. Which one did you choose? Look at the information here and discuss it with your classmates.

The passage that is summarized here is about 550 words in the novel. Summary 1, at 10 words, is 1/55 the length of the original. Does that have enough details to explain what happened?

Summary 2, at 18 words, is about 1/25 of the original. Is that level of detail sufficient?

Summary 3 uses 61 words to summarize the original 550. That's about 1/10 the number of words. How does that level of detail seem?

And summary 4, at 147 words, is a little more than 1/4 of the original text. Does this summary contain too much information, or does it seem just right?

You probably picked summary 3 or summary 4 as the one you liked most. When you write a summary, try to write between 1/10 and 1/4 of the number of words in the original.

Exercise 3. Notice that the summaries that you completed are all written in past tense. It is very common to write a summary in the past tense. You may also write a summary in present tense. Copy the summary that you liked best, changing all of the past verbs to present.

You have seen that summaries can vary in length from 1/10 to 1/4 of the original text and that they can be written in past tense or present tense. In each unit of this text you will do an exercise to help you build your summarizing skills, and you will be asked to summarize a part of the novel on your own.

Response Journals

Response journals help you have a conversation with the novel or a conversation with yourself about the novel. Here is how it works.

As you read, underline passages that you might want to respond to in a journal. Choose a passage that is at least several sentences; from 50 to 100 words is best. Choose a passage that you like or that you don't like, that you think tells something important in the story, or that you don't understand. You may copy a passage that gives you a strong feeling or one that reminds you of something in your life.

You may use a spiral notebook, a composition book, or loose-leaf paper for your journal. After you have chosen and marked the passage in your book, open your response journal and get ready to write. Divide the page in half from top to bottom. Copy the passage that you have chosen onto the left side of the page. Copy carefully, paying attention to format, including indention, capitalization, punctuation, and spelling.

Then on the right side of the page, respond to the passage that you have selected. You may respond in a variety of ways but do not simply summarize the passage. You may tell why you liked the passage or why you didn't like it. You can tell why you chose this passage as an important one in the story and show what you are learning about the characters in the novel. You can make a connection between this passage and something else that you noticed in the novel. You may make predictions based on the ideas in the passage. You may ask questions about parts that you don't understand or about why characters are acting in a certain way. You can tell how the passage made you feel. Or you may relate a story in your life that is similar to something from the passage. Remember: comment, predict, relate, question, but don't summarize.

Good ways to begin your responses are

I think	This passage is	I remember	I agree
I like	This seems	This passage	I don't agree
I don't like	I guess	reminds me	I predict
I wonder	This shows that	I don't understand	
		I'm surprised	

Study these examples of response journals.

Page 13

I heard him move toward me, saw a blur of gray pants and blue shirt. Then, just before he would have touched me, he vanished. The house, the books, everything vanished. Suddenly, I was outdoors kneeling on the ground beneath trees. I was in a green place. I was at the edge of a woods. Before me was a wide tranquil river, and near the middle of that river was a child splashing, screaming . . .

Drowning!

I reacted to the child in trouble.

Response

At first when I read this I thought that Dana was sick. Maybe something in her new house is making her sick. But then when I read on, I remembered that she was going to meet Rufus in this part. Maybe the boy in the river is Rufus. Maybe she is really traveling in an instant to this boy. Is she psychic?

I think this has something to do with Dana's new house. I think she should move back to her old apartment.

I wonder if there is a difference between "vanish" and "disappear."

Page 13

I ran down to the river, waded into the water fully clothed, and swam quickly to the child. He was unconscious by the time I reached him—a small red-haired boy floating, face down. I turned him over, got a good hold on him so that his head was above water, and towed him in. There was a red-haired woman waiting for us on the shore now. Or rather, she was running back and forth crying on the shore. The moment she saw that I was wading, she ran out, took the boy from me and carried him the rest of the way, feeling and examining him as she did.

Response

I think this boy is Rufus because in the first paragraph of this chapter, she says she met Rufus. I have never heard of the name Rufus before. I wonder why the boy's mother doesn't rescue him? Why was she just running on the shore? Maybe she isn't a good mother, or maybe she can't swim and was waiting for help.

I don't know what wading means. I think it is something that you do in water.

Vocabulary Log

As you read your novel, you will find many words that you probably have not seen before. You should try to guess the meaning of a word from what you know about what is happening in the story (the "context"). For example, if someone is eating mush, then mush must be some kind of food. If someone is sleeping on a pallet, then a pallet must be some kind of bed.

Often, however, you want to know exactly what a word means. What kind of food is mush? What kind of bed is a pallet? That's when you need to combine your guessing in context skills with your use of the dictionary. You'll also have to rely on your knowledge of English sentence structure to guess parts of speech such as noun, verb, adjective, and adverb.

The best way to gain practice in this is by keeping a vocabulary log. Here is how it works. For each section of your novel (each unit of this textbook), find at least 10 words that you would be interested in learning more about. They can be words that you just don't know at all or words that you have seen a couple of times and that you are curious about.

You may keep your vocabulary log in a spiral notebook or a composition book, on loose-leaf paper, or on note cards.

Follow this format when you add a word to your list.

Copy the word. Next to the word, write its part of speech in parentheses.

Find any other forms of the word that your dictionary lists (noun, verb, adjective, adverb).

Copy the ONE definition from your dictionary that best fits the way your word is used in the novel.

Copy the sentence in which the word appears from your novel. Underline your word.

When your teacher checks your vocabulary log, he or she will be checking to see that you have chosen the one best definition for the context in which your word appears. The teacher will also check to see that the other forms that you have found are related to your word.

Look at this example from page 9.

comfort (noun)
comfortable (adj.), comfortably (adv.), comfort (verb)
a pleasant style of life in which you have everything you need
And I lost about a year of my life and much of the <u>comfort</u> and secu-
rity I had not valued until it was gone.

Note the format.

word (part of speech)
other forms
definition
sentence from the book

Exercise 1. Complete these vocabulary log entries using words from page 9.

lines 8–9
struggle (_____)
struggle (noun)

_____

The police were shadows who appeared intermittently at my bedside
to ask me questions I had to <u>struggle</u> to understand.

line 13
accident (noun)

_____

an event that happens by chance and is not planned
"<u>Accident,</u>" I heard myself whisper.

line 20
persisted (verb)

_____

to go on in spite of opposition; to persevere

_____

line 23
fault (_____)

_____

_____

"My <u>fault,</u> not Kevin's. Please let me see him."

Now you are ready to begin! Enjoy the novel!

Unit One

Looking Ahead

This unit covers pages 16 through 51 of *Kindred*. In the previous section, you read about Dana's first trip to Rufus. She saved him from drowning in a river. At the beginning of this section, Dana is talking with her husband, Kevin, about her experience. A short time later, she vanishes again.

Freewriting

Before you continue reading, take a few minutes to make some predictions. Respond to each one of these questions with a statement beginning "I think." Use future verbs.

1. Is Kevin going to believe Dana's story, or will he think they are both dreaming?

   _____

   _____

2. Will Dana vanish again?

   _____

   _____

3. Is Dana going to discover why she vanishes and appears in another place?

   _____

   _____

4. Will Dana get to know Rufus better?

   _____

   _____

5. Will Kevin vanish with Dana?

_____

_____

Test Yourself

Complete the following quizzes as you read pages 18 through 51 ("The Fire"). You may use your novel to help you do the quizzes. In fact, it's a good idea to mark the places in your novel where you find the answers.

After you complete the quizzes compare answers with your classmates and discuss the sections of the novel in which you found the answers.

Quiz 1. Pages 18 to 33 (sections 1 and 2). True or false?

__ 1.   When Dana was called back to Rufus, she was still covered in mud from the river.

__ 2.   When her dizziness cleared, Dana found herself in Rufus's kitchen.

__ 3.   Rufus's draperies were on fire.

__ 4.   Dana put out the fire and immediately returned home to her house in California.

__ 5.   Rufus was three or four months older than he had been the last time she saw him.

__ 6.   Dana guessed that she might be in the South by Rufus's accent.

__ 7.   Rufus explained that he "saw" Dana with his eyes closed.

__ 8.   Dana began to realize that she traveled through both distance and time.

__ 9.   Rufus explained that he'd burned down the house once.

__ 10.   Dana discovered that the year was 1915.

__ 11.   Dana discovered that she was in Maryland before slavery was abolished, and she remembered that Maryland was a slave state.

___ 12.   Dana guessed that Rufus was her distant ancestor.

___ 13.   Dana learned that Alice was a slave.

___ 14.   Dana discovered that she was in Baltimore, Maryland.

___ 15.   Dana decided to stay with Rufus in his house.

Quiz 2. Pages 33 to 45 (sections 3 through 5). Circle the best word or words to complete each sentence.

1.   Dana walked to Alice's house in (daytime/nighttime).

2.   Dana became dizzy when a small animal dashed across the road in front of her. She closed her eyes. When she opened them, she was (still on the road/back home with Kevin).

3.   Dana knew that black people were assumed to be slaves unless they carried (money/free papers).

4.   Dana saw eight (white/black) men on horses going toward Alice's house.

5.   The men (whipped/shot) Alice's father, and Alice's mother was (killed/knocked unconscious).

6.   Tom Weylin owns Alice's (mother/father).

7.   Dana told Alice's mother that she was from (New York/California).

8.   When Dana went outside to get the blanket, she met (a patroller/Alice's father).

9.   When the man attacked Dana, she (returned to her home/ran into Alice's house).

10.   Dana was in the past for (days/hours), but in the present only (minutes/hours) passed.

Quiz 3. Pages 45 through 51 (section 6). Complete the following sentences.

1. While Dana slept, Kevin packed a canvas bag and tied it around

   Dana's waist. The tote bag contained _____

   _____.

2. Dana explained to Kevin that patrollers were _____

   _____.

3. Dana and Kevin looked through some books for _____

   _____.

4. Kevin realized that Dana can only come home when she _____

   _____.

5. Dana realized that Rufus calls her to him when he _____

   _____.

Vocabulary

For this section of the novel, add 10 words to your vocabulary log.
Remember, for each word, you should have the following information.

> word (part of speech)
> other forms
> definition
> sentence copied from the novel

Don't forget to choose the one best definition of the word as it is used in
the sentence that you copy.

**Exercise 1. Choosing definitions. Try this exercise to help you choose the
correct definition. Find each of the following words in your novel. After you
understand the context in which the word is used, circle the letter of the best
definition.**

1. Page 12. Now he was closeted there either <u>loafing</u> or thinking
   because I didn't hear his typewriter.

   a. loaf (n.): a portion of baked bread

   b. loaf (v.): to spend time in a lazy way instead of working

2. Page 17. "Hell, I don't blame you for <u>humoring</u> me."

   a. humor (n.): something funny or comical

   b. humor (v.): to go along with someone to make that person happy

3. Page 19. I reached out for the table to <u>steady</u> myself, but before I could touch it, it was gone.

   a. steady (v.): to stabilize or stop from moving

   b. steady (adj.): continuous

4. Page 20. What if I was <u>stranded</u> here—wherever here was?

   a. strand (n.): a single long, thin piece of thread or hair

   b. strand (v.): to leave in a helpless position, often without transportation

5. Page 48. "I've been watching the violence of this time go by on the <u>screen</u> long enough to have picked up a few things."

   a. screen (n.): a movable device designed to hide something or divide a space

   b. screen (n.): a large flat surface on which a picture is projected

Summarizing

Exercise 1. Summaries of fiction are often written in present tense. Here is a summary of pages 33 to 37 (section 3). Reread these pages of the novel and then fill in the blanks with present tense verbs.

In this passage, Dana heads for Alice's house. First she

_____ through some woods, and then she _____ a

road. While she is walking along the road, a small animal

_____ in front of her. She _____ dizzy, but she doesn't

go home. Then she _____ horses approaching, and she hides

in the bushes. She _____ eight white men going toward Alice's

cabin. She follows them. Four of the white men take three people out

of the cabin—a man, a woman, and a child. The child _____

near where Dana is hiding in the bushes. The men _____ the

man from the cabin for a pass, and then they _____ him.

Then they _____ the woman and take the man away.

Exercise 2. Now choose one of the following sections to summarize. Use present verbs in your summary.

1. Pages 19 through 22
2. Pages 24 through 29
3. Pages 38 to 43 (end of section 4)
4. Pages 43 through 51 (sections 5 and 6)

Response Journals

Exercise 1. Summary or response? When you summarize, you simply restate the events of the story. When you respond, you comment about the story. This exercise will give you practice in telling the difference between a summary and a response. Before you do this exercise, reread the part of page 43 that begins "Pain dragged me back to consciousness." After you have understood the passage, read the following paragraphs. Next to each one, write S if you think it is a summary of the passage and write R if you think it is a response to the passage.

__ Dana woke up and saw a man's face above her. She thought that the man was the patroller who had attacked her. Then she realized that it was Kevin and that she was at home.

__ I felt scared when I read this passage. I thought at first that Dana was still being attacked by the patroller. Then when I realized that the man was Kevin, I was afraid that Dana was going to scratch his eyes out or hurt him some other way.

__ This passage reminds me of the time I woke up in the hospital after my operation. I think the pain woke me up the way it dragged Dana back to consciousness. And when I woke up in the hospital, I saw a face above me and got scared at first. Then I recognized my mother's face. I understand a little bit how Dana felt, waking up confused.

__ Dana returned home after the patroller attacked her. When she woke up, Kevin was looking down at her. At first she thought Kevin was a patroller, and she tried to fight him. Then after he said her name she knew it was him, and she knew that she was at home.

Exercise 2. Write response journals for two passages from pages 16 through 51. Think of what is important in this section of the novel when you choose your passages. You might want to write about how Kevin doesn't believe that Dana is traveling to the past or about Dana's realization that Rufus is her ancestor and that she needs to keep him alive. You could also write about how blacks were treated by whites in the early nineteenth century.

Topics for Discussion

By page 51 of *Kindred*, Dana faces a lot of problems. For example, Kevin doesn't believe that she travels to the past. What can she do about this? Can she take a camera to the past with her? Can she bring something home from the past to prove it to Kevin? Think about more problems that Dana faces and discuss the problems and some solutions to each problem with your classmates. Fill in your ideas on this mind map. Write a different problem on each line. Write at least two possible solutions to each problem on the branches.

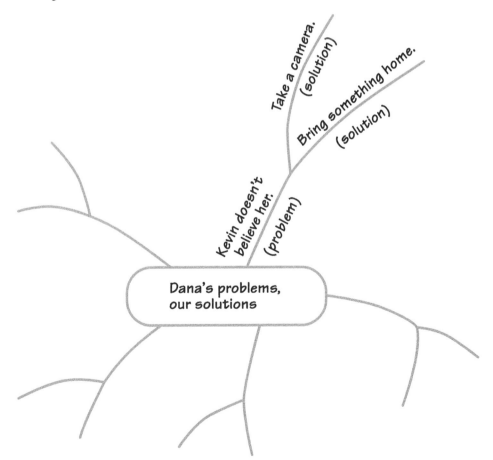

Composition

Choose one of Dana's problems that you discussed with your classmates. Write a short paper in which you explain that problem. Tell why you think it is an important problem. Then give at least two suggestions on how Dana might solve that problem. You can include suggestions even if you don't think they will happen in the book.

Beyond the Novel

On page 27, Dana discovers that she is in the year 1815. Study the following time line to discover what was happening in the United States before and after 1815. Then complete the exercises on pages 17–19.

1775	The American Revolution began in Massachusetts.
1776	The American Continental Congress signed the Declaration of Independence.
1781	The British surrendered at Yorktown to end the American Revolution.
1789	The Constitution of the United States was adopted.
1789	George Washington was elected the first president.
1790	Philadelphia replaced New York as the temporary capital city of the United States.
1791	Washington selected the area that would become Washington, D.C., for the capital.
1791	Vermont became the fourteenth state.
1792	Architect James Hoban designed the White House.
1792	Kentucky became the fifteenth state.
1792	The dollar was selected as the unit of currency for the United States.
1793	Construction on the Capitol Building began.
1800	The government of the United States moved to Washington, D.C.
1800	Thomas Jefferson became the third president.
1803	France sold all of the land between the Mississippi and the Rocky Mountains to the United States.
1805	Explorers Lewis and Clark reached the Pacific Ocean traveling across land.
1812	Territorial disputes led to the War of 1812 with Britain.
1814	The British burned Washington, D.C.
1817	Indiana became the nineteenth state; Mississippi became the twentieth state.
1819	Spain gave Florida to the United States.

1820	The Missouri Compromise allowed Missouri to enter as a slave state (the twenty-fourth state).
1820	Freed slaves left the United States and settled in Liberia.
1822	Denmark Vesey led a slave revolt in Charleston.
1829	Andrew Jackson became the seventh president.
1831	Nat Turner led a slave revolt in Virginia.
1832	The Black Hawk War was the last Indian conflict east of the Mississippi.
1850	California became the thirty-first state.

Exercise 1. Tell what order the following events occurred in by putting 1 before the first, 2 before the second, and 3 before the third.

1. __ Philadelphia was the capital of the United States.

   __ New York was the capital of the United States.

   __ Washington, D.C., was the capital of the United States.

2. __ The Declaration of Independence was signed.

   __ The Constitution was adopted.

   __ The Revolutionary War ended.

3. __ Missouri became a state.

   __ Vermont became a state.

   __ California became a state.

4. __ Thomas Jefferson was president.

   __ Andrew Jackson was president.

   __ George Washington was president.

5. __ The United States purchased the land from the Mississippi to the Rockies.

   __ Spain gave Florida to the United States.

   __ Lewis and Clark reached the Pacific.

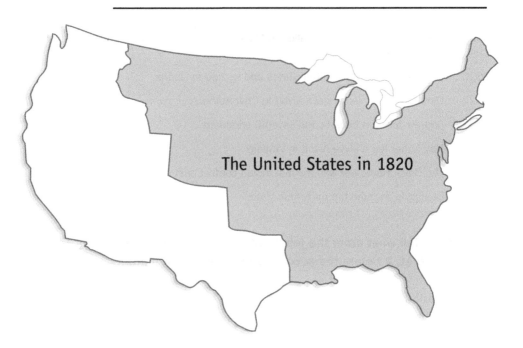

The United States in 1820

A map of the United States looked like this in 1820. Land to the west was owned by Mexico or was unexplored territory.

Exercise 2. We can guess that Rufus was about eight years old in 1815. Keeping that in mind, use the information in the time line to answer these questions.

1. Was Rufus alive when George Washington was president? _____

2. Was Rufus alive when Washington, D.C., became the capital of the country? _____

3. How old was Rufus when the British burned Washington, D.C.?

    _____

4. How old will Rufus be when Nat Turner leads his slave revolt in Virginia? _____

5. Why doesn't Dana tell Rufus that she is from the state of California?

    _____

Exercise 3. Combine pairs of sentences from the time line that seem to go together. Change your first sentence into a clause beginning with "After." Follow the examples.

After the American Revolution began, the Continental Congress signed the Declaration of Independence.

After Washington selected the site of the new capital, James Hoban designed the White House.

_____

_____

_____

_____

Options

Activity 1. Complete this crossword about names and places and events from the novel.

Across

2. Rufus's daughter _____ will be Dana's great-great grandmother.
4. Dana's husband is _____.
6. Rufus lives in _____.
7. Rufus almost drowned in a _____.
8. Dana travels back in _____.
9. Dana has to save _____.
13. A _____ attacked Dana.
14. Easton is a _____ in Maryland.
15. The _____ questioned Kevin while Dana was in the hospital.

Down

1. Dana feels _____ before she vanishes.
3. Dana said that when she lost her arm it was an _____.
5. Dana is from _____.
10. Dana discovered that Rufus is her distant _____.
11. Dana lost an _____ on her last trip home.
12. _____ will be Hagar's mother.

Activity 2. Role play. Role-play the scene when Dana reappears in her house or the scene when Dana and Rufus talk in his bedroom. Work with a group to write a script for the scene. Then choose two students to act out your scene for the class.

Activity 3. Video. Watch a video about time travel, such as *Back to the Future.* Discuss how the time travel in *Kindred* is similar to and different from the time travel in the movie.

Unit Two

Looking Ahead

This unit covers pages 52 through 107 ("The Fall") of *Kindred*. In the previous section, you read about how Dana traveled again to save Rufus, this time from a fire, and how she met Alice. After she returned to the present, she had a long talk with Kevin about her experiences and tried to convince him that what was happening was real.

This section begins with a "flashback." In a flashback, we read about events that happened before the main story in the novel. In this flashback, you will find out how Dana and Kevin met. After the flashback, you will read about another trip to the past to save Rufus's life.

Freewriting

Choose one of the following and freewrite for about 15 minutes.

1. The title of this chapter in *Kindred* is "The Fall." In "The River," Dana saved Rufus from drowning. In "The Fire," Dana put out a fire that could have killed Rufus and his family. From what you know about the chapter titles, what danger do you think Dana might save Rufus from in this chapter?
2. Dana and Kevin met while Dana was working for a temporary employment agency. Dana didn't like her job, but she did it to earn money so that she could write at night. Have you ever had a job that you didn't like? Write about it.
3. Perhaps Kevin will travel to the past with Dana. Will that be good or bad? Will he be able to help her, or will it cause trouble?

Test Yourself

Complete the following quizzes as you read pages 52 through 107. You may use your novel to help you do the quizzes. In fact, it's a good idea to mark the places in your novel where you find the answers.

After you complete the quizzes, compare answers with your classmates and discuss the sections of the novel in which you found the answers.

Quiz 1. Pages 52 to 65 (sections 1 and 2). Complete the following sentences with one or more words.

1. Dana and Kevin met when they were working together in an

    _____.

2. We know that Dana is black. On page 54, we learn that Kevin is

    _____.

3. On the bottom of page 55, we learn that both Dana's and Kevin's

    parents _____.

4. On page 58, Kevin was getting ready to go to the library to look for

    _____.

5. Kevin saw that Dana was about to disappear, and he _____

    _____.

6. Rufus called Dana this time because he had fallen _____

    _____.

7. Kevin told Rufus that Dana was his _____.

8. Starting on page 62, Dana and Kevin tried to explain to Rufus about

    _____.

9. On page 65, Dana told Kevin that the only way he could get home is

    by _____.

Quiz 2. Pages 65 to 74 (section 3). Each of the following statements is false. Correct each statement by changing one or two words.

1. Rufus's mother came to take him home.

2. Rufus wanted Dana to go away.

3. Dana told Tom that she was from California.

4. Tom was very gentle with Rufus.

5. Margaret recognized Kevin.

6. In the hallway, Dana met a girl who couldn't hear.

7.   Sarah liked Margaret.

8.   The white people got the leftovers after the black people ate.

Quiz 3. Pages 76 through 107 (sections 4 through 8). Write a short answer for each of the following. Mark the place in your novel where you find each answer.

1.   What happened to Sarah's other children?

_____

_____

2.   How does Sarah feel about what happened to her family?

_____

_____

3.   On page 77, we learn why Kevin held on to Dana when she was about to disappear. Why did he do that?

_____

_____

4.   What do Dana and Kevin realize in the middle of page 77?

_____

_____

5.   What job did Tom Weylin offer Kevin?

_____

_____

6.   On pages 79 and 80, we learn the story that Kevin told Weylin about why he and Dana were there. What was the story?

_____

_____

7.   How does Margaret feel about Dana? How does she feel about Kevin?

_____

_____

8. What did Dana begin to do on pages 86 and 87?

    _____

    _____

9. What happened to Alice's father?

    _____

    _____

10. What did Tom Weylin ask Dana to do on page 91?

    _____

    _____

11. Whose idea was it to sell Sarah's children?

    _____

    _____

12. What advice did Luke give to Nigel?

    _____

    _____

13. What did Dana start to do on page 98?

    _____

    _____

14. What were the children pretending to do on page 99?

    _____

    _____

15. What did Tom do when he found Dana teaching Nigel in the cook-house?

    _____

    _____

Vocabulary

For this section of the novel, add 10 words to your vocabulary log. Remember, for each word, you should have the following information.

word (part of speech)
other forms
definition
sentence copied from the novel

Don't forget to choose the one best definition of the word as it is used in the sentence that you copy.

Exercise 1. Matching. Match the words about slavery that appear on the left with their correct meaning on the right. Write the letter of the meaning on the line. The page number where the word appears is in parentheses.

___ 1. free papers (p. 58)

___ 2. scythes (p. 67)

___ 3. overseer (p. 67)

___ 4. slaveholder (p. 68)

___ 5. cabins (p. 68)

___ 6. cookhouse (p. 70)

___ 7. master (p. 71)

___ 8. free state (p. 73)

___ 9. attic (p. 82)

___ 10. the quarter (p. 91)

___ 11. field hand (p. 92)

___ 12. driver (p. 96)

a. the title that a slave had to use when he or she talked to a white man

b. an area under the roof of a house where house servants slept

c. a white man who supervised the slaves working in the fields

d. a slave who worked in the field; contrast with "house slave"

e. small buildings, usually with dirt floors, where slaves lived

f. a black man who supervised field hands; contrast with "overseer"

g. a state that did not allow slavery; contrast with "slave state"

h. a group of slave cabins where field slaves lived

i. a document showing that a black person was not a slave

j. a slave owner

k. a small building separated from the main house where slaves cooked for their owners

l. tools with long, curved blades that are used for cutting grain

Summarizing

Exercise 1. In Unit One, you learned that summaries are often written in present tense. You may also summarize fiction in past tense. Practice summarizing in the past tense with this exercise. First, reread from the middle of page 70, where Margaret entered Rufus's room, to the end of that section on page 74. Then fill in the following summary with past tense verbs.

Margaret _____ Dana to leave Rufus's room and go to the cookhouse. Dana _____ down the hallway and met a teenage girl who couldn't talk. That was Carrie. Carrie _____ that Dana was wearing pants, and Dana _____ that everyone thought that she was dressed like a man. Carrie _____ Dana to the cookhouse. Dana _____ several slaves eating in the cookhouse and introduced herself to Sarah, the cook. Sarah _____ Dana some cornmeal mush to eat, and Luke explained that the slaves got to eat the whites' leftovers later on. Dana _____ that she was from New York. She _____ to the slaves why she dressed like a man (because that was what Kevin _____ her to wear) and why she didn't talk like the other slaves (because she was from New York and her mother was a teacher). Then Nigel _____ Dana how Rufus could see her before she got there. Dana _____ she didn't know and that she wished he couldn't.

Exercise 2. Choose one of the following sections to summarize. Use past tense verbs in your summary.

1. Pages 58 through 60
2. Pages 65 through 70
3. Pages 74 to 81 (section 4)
4. Pages 86 through 89
5. Pages 104 (bottom) through 107

Response Journals

Exercise 1. Summary or response? This exercise will give you practice in telling the difference between a summary and a response. Before you do this exercise, reread the passage in the novel on which it is based. The passage begins in the middle of page 94 when Dana enters the cookhouse and ends in the middle of the next page where Sarah says, "It was Marse Tom I spoke to for you." After you have understood the passage, read the following paragraphs. Next to each one, write S if you think it is a summary of the passage and write R if you think it is a response to the passage.

__ Dana went into the cookhouse, and Sarah told her that she had spoken for her that day. Dana wondered if she meant to Margaret, and Sarah told her that she rarely spoke to Margaret. Sarah told Dana that she disliked Margaret so much because Margaret was the one who had decided to sell Sarah's sons. She compared Margaret to Hannah. Sarah thought Hannah was a real lady.

__ In the cookhouse, Dana talked with Sarah and learned that it was Margaret's idea to sell her sons to buy new furniture and dishes. Sarah said that Miss Hannah, Tom's first wife, was a real lady and that Margaret was white trash.

__ It is understandable that Sarah would hate Margaret since it was Margaret's idea to sell Sarah's boys. It seems that Miss Hannah, Tom's first wife, treated Sarah better than Margaret does. Miss Hannah probably treated all of the slaves better than Margaret does.

__ Sarah and Margaret don't have a good relationship. I think Sarah hates Margaret because it was Margaret's idea to sell Sarah's sons. Sarah had a better relationship with Hannah, who was Tom's first wife. It's important to have a good relationship with the person that you work for.

Exercise 2. Write response journals for two passages from pages 60 through 107. From these pages, choose passages that illustrate how the slaves on the Weylin plantation lived or how they were treated by the white slaveholders.

Topics for Discussion

Exercise 1. Review your response journals for this unit and compare your passages with those your classmates chose. What do your passages show about the way the slaves lived in the early nineteenth century in Maryland? Fill in your ideas on this mind map. Write a general idea on each line and then on each branch write a specific example from the novel. Some ideas and examples have been written in for you to help you get started.

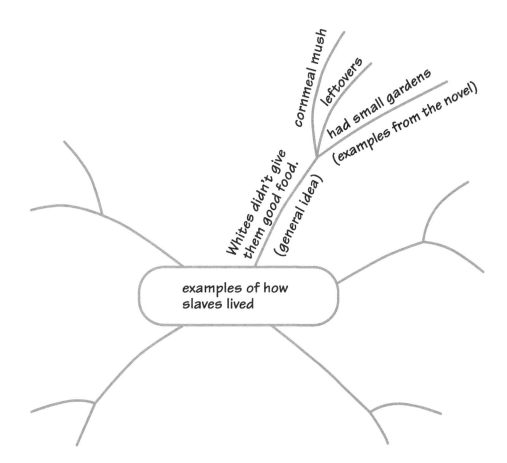

Exercise 2. Venn diagram. While slaves lived in poor conditions, some of the conditions were also shared by their owners. Read this list of nineteenth-century living conditions and put the descriptions in the Venn diagram below. Write the descriptions that applied to slaves in the left-hand circle and the descriptions that applied to slaveholders in the right-hand circle. Where the circles intersect, write descriptions that applied to both.

1. They lived and worked on plantations, far from towns or cities.
2. They didn't have good medical care.
3. They didn't have electricity.
4. They lived in cabins with dirt floors.
5. Their food might be contaminated.
6. They caught diseases from flies and mosquitoes.
7. They could not learn how to read or write.
8. They used outdoor toilets.
9. They lived in fear that slaves would revolt.
10. Mail delivery was slow and unreliable.
11. They used open fires for heating and cooking.
12. They didn't have running water in their houses.
13. They didn't bathe or wash clothes frequently.
14. They could not leave the plantation without a pass.
15. Only boys went to school.

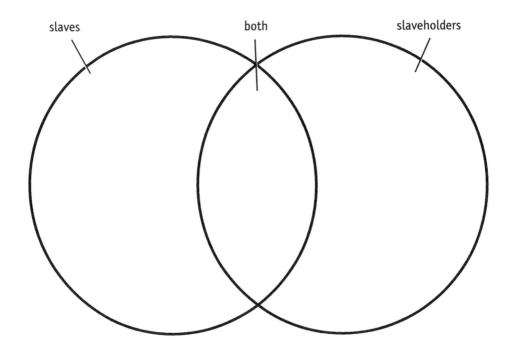

Composition

1. Review the notes that you took on the mind map in your discussion about how slaves lived in the nineteenth century. Write a short paper in which you show how slaves lived. Be sure to support your ideas with specific examples from the novel.
2. Write a short paper in which you compare and contrast how slaves and slaveholders lived in the nineteenth century. In what ways were their lives similar? How were the lives of slaveholders better than the lives of the slaves?

Beyond the Novel

Read this description of the history of slavery and complete the exercises below.

Slavery has existed in many societies since the development of farming over ten thousand years ago. In ancient times, most slaves were prisoners of war. The practice of slavery reached its peak in ancient Greece and Rome, where slaves did most of the work. At one time, one-half of the population of Athens was slaves.

European slavery died out somewhat in the Middle Ages but began to increase in the 1400s as large sugar plantations were created on some Mediterranean islands. At that same time, Portuguese sailors started to explore the coast of Africa, where slavery had been common for centuries. African slaves were usually prisoners of war from rival tribes. The Portuguese began to ship some of these African slaves to Europe to work on the sugar plantations there.

The colonization of the "New World" (North and South America and islands in the Caribbean) by Europeans in the 1500s caused a great expansion in slavery. At first, Spanish and Portuguese settlers enslaved the natives of the lands that they conquered (so-called Indians), but most of those slaves died of European diseases. It was then that they began to import slaves from Africa to the Caribbean and Brazil. In the following century, France, England, and the Netherlands brought more African slaves to work in their new colonies on Caribbean islands. The slaves worked on sugar, cotton, and tobacco plantations.

The first African slaves were brought into North America at Jamestown, Virginia, in 1619. The first Africans in North America were probably indentured servants, who worked a set number of years in exchange for their freedom. However, by 1670, all Africans in the English colonies were considered to be slaves unless they could prove otherwise.

From the 1500s to the middle of the 1800s, Europeans brought 12,000,000 slaves from Africa to the New World. Nearly 20 percent of those died on the voyage. Of those who lived, most were shipped to islands in the Caribbean and to South America, especially Brazil. Six percent of the slaves brought from Africa were sent to North America; first to the English colonies there and, after independence, to the United States.

People may be forced into slavery in several ways. They may be kidnapped or taken as prisoners in a war. Slavery can result from debt or poverty or as a penalty for a crime. Other times, children are traded into slavery because of poverty or as a form of female infanticide. And finally, in slave systems that have existed for a number of years, one may be born into slavery.

Kidnapping was by far the most common manner in which Africans were forced into slavery in the New World. African slaves formed part of a great triangle of trade in the 1600s and 1700s. Ships left Europe loaded with manufactured goods including weapons, metal, cloth, and liquor. They sailed to Africa, where they traded their goods for slaves. They then sailed for America, where they traded the slaves for raw materials such as cotton, which they carried back to Europe.

The triangle trade ended in the early 1800s when most European countries abolished international slave trade. The abolition of international trade did not reduce slavery in the United States. While slavery slowly died out in the North, where the economy was based on small farms and industries, in the South, large numbers of laborers were needed to work on the many cotton and tobacco plantations. Slaveholders conducted "slave breeding" and continued to buy and sell the offspring of slaves.

In 1790, there were 700,000 slaves in the United States. By 1830, there were 3,000,000, and by 1860, 6,000,000. The slaves made up about one-third of the population of the slave states. However, only one-fourth of the whites in those states owned slaves or belonged to families who owned them.

By 1860, the map of the United States looked like the one on the opposite page, with 18 free states and 15 slave states. Slaves were also held in many territories west of the Mississippi.

Free and Slave States in 1860

MAINE

DAKOTA
TERRITORY

WISCONSIN

MICHIGAN

VT.
N.H.
MASS.
CONN. R.I.

MINNESOTA

NEW YORK

NEBRASKA
TERRITORY

IOWA

INDIANA

OHIO

PENNSYLVANIA
MASON-DIXON LINE

N.J.

ILLINOIS

DEL. – 2,000
MD. – 87,000

KANSAS
TERRITORY

MISSOURI
115,000

KENTUCKY
225,000

VIRGINIA
491,000

NORTH
CAROLINA
331,000

INDIAN
TERRITORY

ARKANSAS
111,000

TENNESSEE
276,000

MISSISSIPPI
437,000

SOUTH
CAROLINA
402,000

TEXAS
183,000

ALABAMA
435,000

GEORGIA
462,000

LOUISIANA
332,000

FLORIDA
62,000

☐ Free States   ☐ Slave States

This map shows slave states and free states in the eastern United States in 1860. California and Oregon, on the West Coast, were also free states, but all of the other territories in the West were open to slavery.

Exercise 1. Ordering. Tell in which order the following events occurred by putting 1 before the first, 2 before the second, and 3 before the third.

1. __ Portuguese sailors explored the coast of Africa.

    __ Portuguese sailors brought slaves to islands in the

    Mediterranean.

    __ Sugar plantations were established on Mediterranean islands.

2. __ Slaveholders "bred" slaves and sold their offspring.

    __ European slaves arrived from Africa in the triangle trade.

    __ European countries abolished the international slave trade.

3.   __ Slavery died out somewhat in the Middle Ages.

__ Slavery originated with the discovery of farming ten thousand
years ago.

__ Slavery reached its peak in ancient Greece.

**Exercise 2. True or false. Read each of the following and decide if it is true or
false. Look back at the reading if you can't remember the information.**

__ 1.   Slavery has existed for thousands of years.

__ 2.   Slavery began in ancient Greece.

__ 3.   Slavery increased in the Middle Ages.

__ 4.   Portuguese sailors brought African slaves to Europe.

__ 5.   Most African slaves were brought to North America.

__ 6.   The international slave trade was abolished in 1750.

__ 7.   African slaves were part of a triangle of trade that included raw
materials and manufactured goods.

__ 8.   By 1860, about one-third of the people in the slave states were
slaves.

**Exercise 3. True or false. Study the map and decide if each of the following is
true or false.**

__ 1.   Virginia was a free state.

__ 2.   Maryland was a slave state.

__ 3.   Mississippi had the largest number of slaves.

__ 4.   Texas didn't have any slaves.

__ 5.   New York was a free state.

__ 6.   Pennsylvania had a lot of slaves.

__ 7.   Virginia had the greatest number of slaves.

__ 8.   Arkansas was a slave state.

Options

Activity 1. Matching. You met, learned about, or got to know better 10 characters in this section of the novel. Match the names with their descriptions.

___ 1. Kevin

___ 2. Buz

___ 3. Nigel

___ 4. Tom

___ 5. Luke

___ 6. Margaret

___ 7. Carrie

___ 8. Sarah

___ 9. Miss Hannah

___ 10. Mr. Jennings

a. worked in the auto-parts warehouse with Dana and Kevin.

b. was the schoolmaster.

c. worked in the cookhouse and was Carrie's mother.

d. played with Rufus and was Luke's son.

e. was Sarah's daughter who couldn't talk but could hear.

f. was Dana's husband, or her owner if you believed his story.

g. was Tom's first wife; she died.

h. was Rufus's father and the owner of the plantation.

i. was Nigel's father and worked closely with Tom.

j. was Rufus's mother and Tom's second wife.

This wood engraving, "A Slave Auction at the South," appeared in a magazine in 1861. (Courtesy of the Library of Congress)

Activity 2. Video. Borrow the video *Roots* from your local library or video rental store and watch all or part of it. Compare scenes from *Roots* with some scenes from *Kindred*.

Activity 3. Research. Look up the term *slavery* in an encyclopedia in your local library. Read the first part of the entry, in which slavery as a general concept is described. Then write a short paper giving examples of slavery from many societies or describe a situation that exists today that might be considered slavery. Tell why you think the situation can be or cannot be considered slavery.

Activity 4. Role play. Role-play the scene when Dana and Kevin appear together in the past after Rufus has fallen out of the tree. Dana and Kevin have to explain to Rufus who they are and where they are from. Work with a group to write a script for the scene. Then choose three students to act out your scene for the class.

Unit Three

Looking Ahead

This unit covers pages 108 through 148 (approximately one-half of the chapter entitled "The Fight")(sections 1 through 7). In the previous section, Kevin traveled to the past with Dana. Now Dana has come home after Tom beat her for teaching Nigel how to read.

This section begins with another flashback. In this flashback, Dana tells about how she and Kevin got married, in spite of the protests of both families. Following the flashback, Dana is at home for a few days before she is called to save Rufus again.

Freewriting

Choose one of the following topics and write for about 15 minutes.

1. On the bottom of page 107, Kevin is running toward Dana as Tom is beating her. Dana and Kevin both know that she is probably going to return home to 1976. Do you think Kevin reached her in time and came home with her? Why? Do you think he stayed in the past? If he stayed in the past without her, what dangers does he face?

2. In "The Fight," you will read about how both Kevin's and Dana's families opposed their interracial marriage. How do people in your culture usually react to interracial marriage? What about marriages between people of different religions?

3. Dana's and Kevin's families objected to their marriage. Write about a couple that you know who got married in spite of their families' objections. How did the marriage turn out?

Test Yourself

Quiz 1. Pages 108 to 112 (section 1). Circle the word or words that best complete the following statements.

1. Dana (liked/didn't like) typing Kevin's manuscripts.

2. At first, Kevin thought that his sister would (love/hate) Dana.

3. After Kevin talked with his sister, he found that she (approved of/didn't approve of) Kevin's marrying Dana.

4. Dana thought that her aunt accepted the idea of her marrying Kevin because their children would (have lighter skin/have darker skin).

5. Dana's uncle wanted Dana to marry (someone like him/someone like Kevin).

6. Dana and Kevin got married in (Los Angeles/Las Vegas).

Quiz 2. Pages 112 to 117 (section 2). Complete the following sentences with facts from the story.

1. When Dana woke up, she was lying _____.

2. Dana realized that Kevin was _____.

3. Dana found a new denim bag to carry. In it, she put _____ _____.

4. Dana felt confused. She felt caught between _____ and _____ _____.

5. Dana learned that she had spent _____ months in the past but had come back home the same day she had left.

6. Dana needed someone to go out and buy groceries for her, so she called _____.

7. Dana was still afraid to go out of the house because _____ _____.

8. When Dana's cousin saw the bruises on Dana, she thought that Kevin _____ and told Dana to call _____.

9. While Dana was home, she read _____.

Quiz 3. Pages 117 to 148 (sections 3 through 7). Each of the following statements is false. Correct each one by changing one or more words.

1. Dana was called back to the past because Rufus was being beaten up by Alice.

2. The black man killed Rufus.

3. Dana discovered that Alice and Rufus were married.

4. Dana also discovered that Isaac was a slave who belonged to Tom.

5. Alice told Dana that Kevin was still waiting for her at Tom's house.

6. Alice and Isaac decided to go back to the plantation.

7. Dana convinced Rufus to say that Isaac had beaten him up.

8. If Alice is caught helping a slave escape, she can continue to be free.

9. On page 124, Dana learned that Rufus really hates Alice.

10. When Dana got to the Weylin plantation, she was met at first by Tom; then, she saw Sarah.

11. Dana learned from Tom that Kevin had traveled west.

12. Sarah told Dana that Margaret had died.

13. Dana heard about Nigel and Carrie's wedding. Dana remembered that slaves' marriage ceremonies often included jumping over a bucket. Slave marriages were always legal.

14. Rufus told Dana that Tom was unfair.

15. Dana found some letters in Rufus's desk. She learned that Kevin had gone first to Baltimore. Then he went to New York and Boston. He was talking about going to New Hampshire.

16. Before Margaret went to Baltimore, she had another baby.

17. Dana learned that Luke had run away once and that Nigel had been sold.

18. Rufus let Dana keep the history book.

19. Rufus promised to burn the letter to Kevin if Dana would burn the map, too.

20. Alice and Isaac ran away successfully.

21. Sarah liked talking about escaping.

22. The judge bought Alice after she was captured.

Vocabulary

For this section of the novel, add 10 words to your vocabulary log. Remember, for each word, you should have the following information.

word (part of speech)
other forms
definition
sentence copied from the novel

Don't forget to choose the one best definition of the word as it is used in the sentence that you copy.

Exercise 1. Choosing definitions. Try this exercise to help you choose the correct definition. Find each of the following words in your novel. After you understand the context in which the word is used, circle the letter of the best definition.

1. Page 63. "We do," I <u>admitted.</u> "Some things. Not very much. We're not historians."

   a. admit (v.): to allow to enter

   b. admit (v.): to confess; to say the truth

2. Page 67. I glanced at Kevin, not wanting to contradict anything he had said. He gave me a slight nod, and I <u>assumed</u> I was free to make up my own lies.

   a. assume (v.): to suppose; believe something is true without knowing

   b. assume (v.): to take on (responsibility)

3. Pages 70–71. Just then, a young black girl in a long blue dress came out of a door at the other end of the hall. She came toward me, staring at me with open <u>curiosity.</u>

   a. curiosity (n.): a desire to know about things

   b. curiosity (n.): something unusual that arouses interest

4. Page 77. "Then when you were here, I realized that you probably couldn't get back without me. That means if we're separated, you're <u>stranded</u> here for years, maybe for good."

    a. strand (n.): a single long, thin piece of thread or hair

    b. strand (v.): to leave in a helpless position, often without transportation

    c. strand (n.): a beach

5. Page 117. Then it <u>occurred</u> to me that he might really be doing just that–killing the only person who might be able to help me find Kevin.

    a. occur (v.): to take place, happen

    b. occur (v.): to come to mind, suggest itself

6. Page 125. "I said we were dangerous to each other. That's more a reminder than a threat." Actually, it was more a <u>bluff.</u>

    a. bluff (v.): to pretend or mislead someone in order to get something

    b. bluff (n.): a steep cliff

    c. bluff (n.): a pretense; the act of pretending in order to intimidate someone

7. Page 131. I sponged Rufus off as best I could and bandaged his ribs with pieces of cloth that Nigel brought me. The ribs were very <u>tender</u> on the left side.

    a. tender (adj.): sore and painful

    b. tender (adj.): soft, delicate, and gentle

    c. tender (n.): a person who tends something

8. Page 134. I stayed up with Rufus until he <u>managed</u> to fall asleep. The aspirins did seem to help.

    a. manage (v.): to direct or control something

    b. manage (v.): to succeed in doing something that is difficult

9. Page 134. "If I tell you to do something, and he doesn't like it, he'll come to me about it. He won't whip you for following *my* orders. He's a <u>fair</u> man."

    a. fair (adj.): just or equitable to all parties

    b. fair (adj.): moderately good; not very good or very bad

10. Page 141. "You know who Vesey was?" "Yes." A freedman who had <u>plotted</u> to free others violently.

    a. plot (n.): the series of events in a story

    b. plot (v.): to plan in secret

Summarizing

Exercise 1. A summary is often a retelling of the events in the plot. Practice putting some of the events from this section in order. Read the following groups of sentences. Put the number 1 next to the event that happened first, 2 next to the second, and 3 next to the third.

1. __ Dana and Kevin told their families about each other.

    __ Dana and Kevin moved into a bigger new apartment.

    __ Dana and Kevin got married in Las Vegas.

2. __ Dana took a warm bath.

    __ Dana woke up at home.

    __ Dana slept.

3. __ Dana's cousin advised her to report Kevin to the police.

    __ Dana tried to write about what had happened to her, but she couldn't.

    __ Dana called her cousin and asked her to buy groceries.

4. __ Rufus raped Alice.

    __ Isaac beat Rufus up.

    __ Alice and Isaac ran away.

5. __ Dana, Tom, and Nigel brought Rufus back to the house.

    __ Tom told Dana that Kevin had gone somewhere in the North.

    __ Tom recognized Dana.

6. __ Margaret went to live in Baltimore.

    __ Margaret was sick, fought with Tom a lot, and went kind of crazy.

    __ Margaret had twins who died shortly after they were born.

7. __ Rufus promised to mail Dana's letter to Kevin.

    __ Rufus made Dana burn the book.

    __ Rufus made Dana burn the map.

Exercise 2. Choose one of the following sections of the novel to summarize. Use past tense verbs in your summary.

1. Pages 108 to 112 (section 1)
2. Pages 112 to 117 (section 2)
3. Pages 117 through 120 (section 3)
4. Pages 126 to 131 (section 5)
5. Pages 140 to 143
6. Pages 143 to 148 (section 7)

Response Journals

Exercise 1. Summary or response? Before you do this exercise, reread the passages on which it is based. Passage 1 is on page 134, lines 13 through 21. (From "I had gotten him a breakfast tray . . ." to "Daddy'd do some cussin' if he came in here and found us eating together.") Passage 2 is on page 135, lines 19 through 31. (From "Wait. Let me tell it all . . ." to " . . . I want to find my husband.")

Next to each of the following, write S if you think it is a summary of the passage. Write R if you think it is a response to the passage.

Passage 1

__ Sarah prepared a large breakfast for Rufus, and Dana brought it up to him. Dana shared Rufus's breakfast with him in his room. Rufus said that Tom wouldn't like it if he found the two of them eating together.

__ Dana wasn't supposed to share Rufus's breakfast because blacks and whites were not permitted to eat together. I saw a television program recently that showed how even in this century, blacks and whites were not permitted to eat in the same restaurant. I learned that some of the first civil rights protests were about integrating lunch counters.

__ I know that Sarah prepared a large meal because she knew that Dana needed to eat, too. I think it is terrible that Tom would get angry if he found Dana eating with Rufus. He knows that Dana saved Rufus's life, and he should let them eat together.

Passage 2

__ I don't understand how Dana spends a long time in the past (as long as two months) and time doesn't pass for her at home. I guess this is "science fiction." Does Dana look older when she gets home? Will Kevin look five years older when she finds him?

__ Dana is explaining to Rufus that she comes to him and stays for hours or even months but that in 1976 time doesn't pass. She is gone from her time for only a few minutes or hours.

__ Dana told Rufus that she came to him twice on one day in 1976. First, she rescued him from a river, and then she put out the fire in his room when he was a few years older. Then she returned on the next day in 1976, but several years had passed. Finally, after eight days at home, she returned again.

Exercise 2. Write response journals for two passages from pages 120 to 148 (sections 4 through 7).

Topics for Discussion

Exercise 1. Mind maps. At this point in the novel, several characters know Dana well. However, the various characters know different things about Dana and have different opinions about her. Work with your classmates to fill out the following mind maps. Write a general idea on each line. Write examples on each branch.

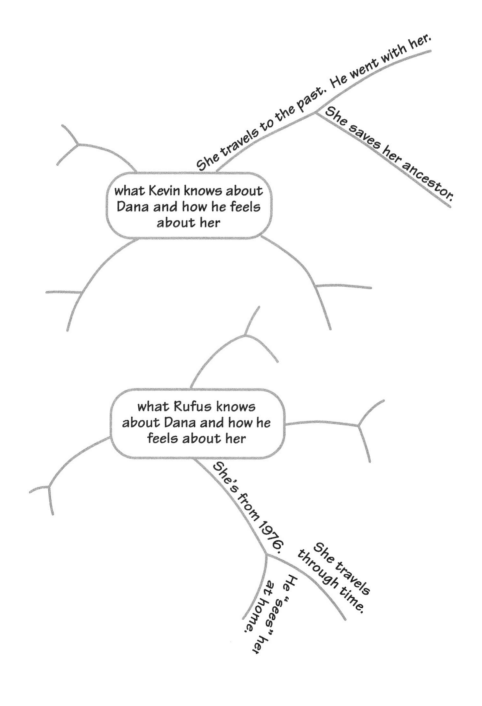

She travels to the past. He went with her.

She saves her ancestor.

what Kevin knows about Dana and how he feels about her

what Rufus knows about Dana and how he feels about her

She's from 1976.

She travels through time.

He "sees" her at home.

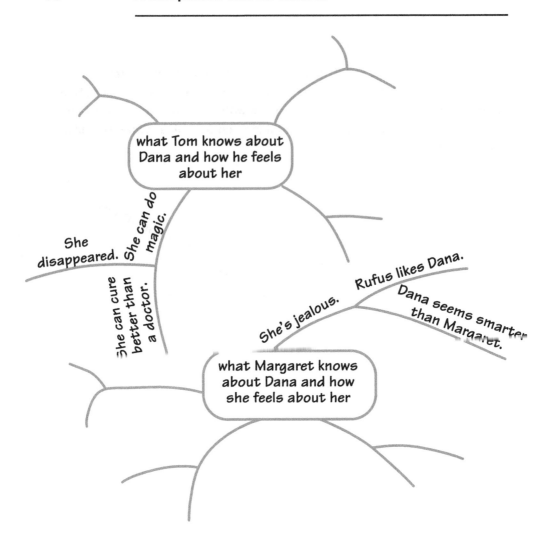

Exercise 2. Venn diagram. Dana is important to both Rufus and Kevin. Read this list of descriptions and put them in the Venn diagram on page 47. Write the descriptions that apply to Rufus in the right part and the ones that apply to Kevin in the left part. Where the circles intersect, write the descriptions that apply to both.

He thinks Dana is smart.
He loves Dana.
He relies on Dana to save his life.
He knows that Dana travels through time.
He met Dana when he was a boy.
He knows that Rufus is Dana's ancestor.
He knows that Dana can write.
He likes to spend time with Dana.
Some members of his family don't like Dana.

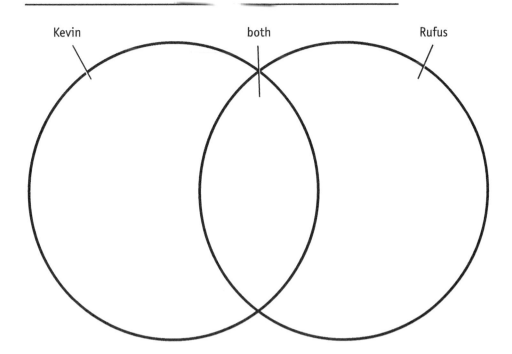

Kevin   both   Rufus

Composition

Introduction to point-of-view writing: *Kindred* is written from Dana's point of view. That means that we readers see the action and the other characters through Dana's eyes.

It is often interesting to imagine a story through the eyes of another character. Of course, you must "suspend disbelief" when you do this. "Suspend disbelief" means that you stop (suspend) not believing (disbelief). You suspend disbelief when you believe that Dana and Kevin travel through time. You do this in order to understand the novel. In point-of-view writing, you may have to believe that a slave who is illiterate can write or that a young child can read and write. Once you suspend disbelief you can write about a novel from many points of view.

Exercise 1. Read the following letter and tell who you think wrote it. Whose point of view is this? What details help you to guess?

Dear Cousin,

    I want to tell you about a woman who comes to our plantation sometimes. She is black like us, but she doesn't talk like us. In fact, she knows how to read and write. She said that she comes from a free state and that her mother was a teacher, but I don't know if I believe her. Besides, you know how I get scared thinking about things like free states and escaping. She even tried to tell me once about slaves who escape to free states, but I didn't want to listen to her. It's dangerous to talk about escaping. Then she wanted to tell me about how runaway slaves wrote books. I couldn't believe this, and anyway, you know I don't like hearing about books and reading. That all makes me very nervous!

Well, this woman's name is Dana. She helps me in the cookhouse sometimes. You know, when she first came here, she didn't know anything about cooking. I have taught her a lot. But most of the time when she is here she helps Rufus. She even talked him out of saying that Isaac beat him up. I told her that I hope she stays around for a while because she seems to be a good influence on him. But she does disappear all of a sudden. I don't understand where she goes when she disappears. I hope you can come to our plantation some day and meet her. Please write soon.

Your cousin,

_____

Exercise 2. Point-of-view writing. Imagine that you are one of the characters listed below. Write a letter to a cousin whom you haven't seen for a long time. Tell your cousin about Dana.

Rufus   Kevin   Margaret   Tom

Beyond the Novel

Read this description of how slaves lived and how some escaped and complete the exercises below.

The slaves who came to North America were brought from the area of Africa that stretches from the Senegal River in the north to the southern part of Angola. They represented many ethnic and linguistic groups, including Wolof, Fulani, Hausa, and Kongo. These ethnic groups were mixed in America, forcing the slaves to use the language of their masters to communicate. Slaves also adopted many of the social customs of their masters, as well as the Christian religion, which they mixed with African rituals.

Slaves who worked in the American South can be broken roughly into two groups: field slaves and house slaves. Field slaves had a much harder

This pencil drawing depicts slaves in a slave cabin in Virginia.
(Courtesy of the Library of Congress.)

life than house slaves. They lived in cabins with dirt floors and had no more
than hay and rags for beds. They worked long hours, often from sunup to
sundown. On the other hand, the slaves who served the masters in their
homes tended to work shorter hours and live in the house with the masters. While they had to put up with the whims of their masters more than
field slaves did, these house slaves were the ones who were most likely to
be freed by their masters.

Beginning in the middle of the 1600s, slaves had to live under rules
called "slave codes." These declared that slaves could not receive an education, meet together in groups, or move freely without permission, could
not marry, own property, or earn their freedom, and could not own weapons
or testify in court. However, some owners who hoped to encourage loyalty
among their slaves often promised them money or freedom, or allowed
them to marry, or gave them gifts.

Other owners relied on punishments to control their slaves. They
whipped them or withheld food as a punishment. Others threatened to sell
members of the slaves' families as punishment.

Slaves protested in several ways. They disobeyed orders or pretended to be sick and unable to work. They secretly destroyed property. And they ran away, hoping to escape to a free state or to Canada.

By the middle of the 1800s, slaves were escaping to the North with the help of other slaves, free blacks, and some whites in both the North and the South. This informal system of help for escaping slaves was called the "Underground Railroad." The Underground Railroad was not under the ground, and it was not a real railroad. It was called "underground" because it was secret, and it was called a "railroad" because it consisted of "stations" or safe places where the slaves could stop along the way. "Conductors" helped the slaves at each "station" as they headed north.

Slaves who escaped generally were on their own through the South, where they traveled by foot at night and hid during the day. Once they made it north to Indiana, Ohio, or Pennsylvania, they were helped by Quakers and other white abolitionists who gave them food, clothing, directions, and places to hide.

Even after the slaves reached the North, they were not safe. This was because of Fugitive Slave Laws, which had been in effect since the end of the eighteenth century. The Fugitive Slave Laws gave slave owners the right to reclaim runaway slaves in other states just by presenting proof of ownership to a judge. This meant that Canada was the first place where many escaped slaves finally found freedom, and many routes on the Underground Railroad led to the Canadian border.

Thousands of slaves escaped on the Underground Railroad before slavery was finally abolished at the end of the Civil War in 1865.

Exercise 1. Multiple choice. Circle the letter of the best response.

1. The slaves who came to North America from Africa

    a. spoke several African languages.

    b. spoke one African language.

    c. already spoke English.

2. According to the reading, which of the following is true?

    a. Field slaves had better living conditions than house slaves.

    b. House slaves had better living conditions than field slaves.

    c. Field slaves and house slaves had about the same living conditions.

$100 REWARD!

RANAWAY

From the undersigned, living on Current River, about twelve miles above Doniphan,

in Ripley County, Mo., on 2nd of March, 1860, A NE GRO MAN, about 30 years old, weighs about 160 pounds; high forehead, with a scar on it; had on brown pants and coat very much worn, and an old black wool hat; shoes size No. 11.

The above reward will be given to any person who may apprehend this said negro out of the State; and fifty dollars if apprehended in this State outside of Ripley county, or $25 if taken in Ripley county.

APOS TUCKER.

This poster was produced by a slave owner who hoped to reclaim a runaway slave under the Fugitive Slave Laws. (Courtesy of the Library of Congress.)

3. Which of the following was *not* prohibited by the "slave codes"?

   a. bearing children with other slaves

   b. earning one's freedom

   c. getting married

4. Which of the following is something that slave owners did to encourage loyalty?

   a. They allowed slaves to learn to read and write.

   b. They allowed slaves to travel freely.

   c. They allowed slaves to marry other slaves.

5. The "Underground Railroad" was

    a. underground.

    b. secret.

    c. a railroad.

6. The Underground Railroad used code names borrowed from real railroads, including

    a. "engine" and "caboose."

    b. "car" and "engineer."

    c. "station" and "conductor."

7. Which of the following did *not* help slaves escape on the Underground Railroad?

    a. Quakers

    b. abolitionists

    c. slave owners

8. Why did many runaway slaves go to Canada?

    a. because there were better jobs there

    b. because if they stayed in the United States they could be returned to their owners under the "Fugitive Slave Laws"

    c. because they liked the climate

9. What did a slave owner have to do in order to reclaim a runaway slave?

    a. show proof of ownership to a judge

    b. pay a fine

    c. kidnap him or her

10. How many slaves escaped on the Underground Railroad?

    a. hundreds

    b. thousands

    c. millions

Options

Activity 1. Name search. Look for 12 names of characters in this puzzle. The names can be horizontal or vertical.

```
A  M  I  S  S  H  A  N  N  A  H  X
C  A  R  R  I  E  R  U  F  S  A  B
P  R  A  N  D  A  T  M  K  A  I  U
C  G  D  A  N  V  E  K  R  R  N  Z
M  A  M  A  K  E  V  I  N  A  R  T
T  R  R  U  F  F  R  X  I  H  N  T
S  E  J  E  N  N  U  R  G  B  O  B
N  T  O  M  I  T  F  R  E  L  A  M
W  E  Y  L  O  D  U  U  L  U  K  E
S  U  S  I  R  A  S  S  I  N  G  T
P  M  R  J  E  N  N  I  N  G  S  L
A  B  L  O  M  A  J  O  N  C  D  E
```

Activity 2. Visit your public library and check out a book on the Underground Railroad. The best place to look is in the children's or young adults' section. You may want to read a fictionalized account of a slave family's escape or choose one of the excellent picture books by children's authors Faith Ringgold, David A. Adler, or Jeanette Winter.

Activity 3. Study the cover of the novel *Kindred.* What do you think the artist who created this cover was trying to depict? Draw a picture to replace the one on the cover. What does your picture mean?

Unit Four

Looking Ahead

This unit covers pages 148 through 188 (sections 8 through 16), or the second half of "The Fight." In this section, Dana remains in the past. Rufus has recovered from his fight with Isaac, and Isaac and Alice have been caught. While Dana tends to Alice's wounds, she learns that Isaac has been sold to a trader who was headed to Mississippi.

While Dana helps Alice recover, she continues to try to find Kevin, who has traveled to the North.

Freewriting

Choose one of the following topics and write for about 15 minutes.

1. In this section of the novel, Dana is waiting for Kevin to return to the Weylin plantation. She has asked Rufus to mail a letter to Kevin. What else do you think Dana can do to find Kevin? Give Dana some advice in your writing.

2. In this section of the novel, Alice is badly injured after she is captured. Dana takes care of her until she is strong again. Write about a time when you were injured. How did you hurt yourself? Who took care of you?

3. Carrie has her baby in this section of the novel, and Sarah helps with the delivery. While Sarah is helping Carrie, Dana takes over in the kitchen and prepares a full meal for the Weylins. The meal is described on page 159. This is the first time Dana has prepared a meal in this unfamiliar kitchen, and she is satisfied with her work. Write about one of the first times you cooked a meal. When was it? What did you cook? How did you feel after you did it?

Test Yourself

Quiz 1. Pages 148 through 168 (sections 8 through 11). Each of the following statements is false. Correct each one by changing one or more words.

1. Rufus and Dana were cleaning the bite wounds caused by the horses that bit Alice when the patrollers caught her.

2. Isaac went back to work for the judge.

3. Rufus told Dana that he had not mailed her letter to Kevin.

4. They cut off Isaac's toes to punish him.

5. Nigel ran away once, and Rufus wanted him to be sold South.

6. Dana and Alice helped Sarah deliver Carrie's baby.

7. Alice discovered that she was still free.

8. Carrie and Nigel had a daughter and named her Jewel.

9. Nigel knew that Tom Weylin was happy now because Carrie and he had a real family.

10. Tom Weylin learned that Rufus had written a letter to Kevin.

11. Rufus wanted Dana to convince Alice to run away.

12. Alice decided to run away again rather than go to Rufus.

Quiz 2. Pages 168 through 188 (sections 12 through 16). Circle the best word or words to complete each sentence.

1. Dana decided to travel to the (North/South) to find Kevin.

2. Alice showed Dana that (Tom/Rufus) hadn't mailed her letters to Kevin.

3. Dana left the plantation around (midnight/noon).

4. Dana had traveled for several (hours/days) before Tom and Rufus found her.

5. Tom kicked Dana in the face, and Dana passed out. When she awoke, she was (at home in California/thrown over Rufus's horse).

6.   (Jake Edwards/Tom Weylin) whipped Dana in the barn.

7.   Dana didn't go home to California during the whipping because she knew it (would/wouldn't) kill her.

8.   Liza (was beaten by Alice, Tess, and Carrie/fell and hurt herself) because she was the one who told Tom Weylin that Dana had run away.

9.   Rufus showed Dana a letter that Kevin had sent to (him/Tom).

10.   Jake Edwards sent (Tess/Alice) to work in the fields.

11.   Kevin arrived, and he and Dana decided to (stay at the plantation/leave right away).

12.   Rufus threatened to shoot Dana because he wanted her to (stay/leave).

Quiz 3. Pages 148 through 188 (sections 8 through 16). Read the quotations on the left. You may want to open your book and reread some of the page where the quotation appears. Then match the quotation with the description of what the character is saying that appears on the right.

___ 1.   p. 148 "He'd be dead if I'd spoken up."

___ 2.   p. 151 "He always said he'd free me in his will, but he didn't."

___ 3.   p. 152 "Tried to run once. Followed the Star."

___ 4.   p. 156 "What's it like to be a slave?"

___ 5.   p. 161 "Thank you, Marse Tom. Yes sir. Sure do thank you. Fine clothes. yes, sir . . ."

___ 6.   p. 168 "I'm lying. I can't run again."

a.   Sarah explains that her previous master, who was the father of her oldest child, promised to give her her freedom when he died.

b.   Tom tells Rufus that it is Rufus's fault, not Kevin's, that Dana tried to run away.

c.   Nigel thanks Tom for the gifts Tom gave him after Jude was born. Later, Nigel tells Dana that Tom is happy about the birth of Nigel and Carrie's baby because their baby will be Tom's slave too.

___ 7.   p. 173 "You're damning the wrong man."

___ 8.   p. 178 "Fell on the stairs."

___ 9.   p. 179 "I wanted to keep you here."

___ 10.   p. 187 "Damn you, you're not leaving me!"

d.   Liza, the sewing woman, gives the official explanation of how she got the injuries that she received from Alice, Tess, and Carrie after she told Tom that Dana had run away.

e.   Rufus explains that Isaac would have been killed if Rufus had told the patrollers that Isaac had beaten him up.

f.   Rufus tells Dana why he had lied to her about mailing her letters to Kevin.

g.   As Alice begins to get better and doesn't yet know that Rufus has bought her, she asks Dana what it's like to be a slave.

h.   Rufus explains why he is willing to shoot Dana.

i.   Nigel says that he ran away once by following the North Star.

j.   Alice explains why she will go to Rufus, since she can't run away again.

Vocabulary

For this section of the novel, add 10 words to your vocabulary log. Remember, for each word, you should have the following information.

> word (part of speech)
> other forms
> definition
> sentence copied from the novel

Don't forget to choose the one best definition of the word as it is used in the sentence that you copy.

Exercise 1. Word forms. Use your dictionary to find other forms of these words from pages 148 through 168. Other forms have close to the same meaning but are used differently in sentences. The first one is done for you.

nausea (n.), p. 148   nauseate (v.)   nauseous (adj.)

information (n.), p. 148   _____ (v.)   _____ (adj.)

wearily (adv.), p. 149   _____ (adj.)   _____ (n.)

gentle (adj.), p. 150   _____ (adv.)   _____ (n.)

patient (adj.), p. 150   _____ (adv.)   _____ (n.)

comfortable (adj.), p. 150   _____ (adv.)   _____ (n.)

                           _____ (v.)

important (adj.), p. 153   _____ (n.)   _____ (adv.)

silence (n.), p. 154   _____ (adj.)   _____ (adv.)

continued (v.), p. 154   _____ (n.)   _____ (adj.)

                           _____ (adv.)

angry (adj.), p. 157   _____ (adv.)   _____ (n.)

                           _____ (v.)

bitterly (adv.), p. 160   _____ (adj.)   _____ (n.)

relaxed (v.), p. 164   _____ (n.)

curious (adj.), p. 167   _____ (adv.)   _____ (n.)

difference (n.), p. 167   _____ (v.)   _____ (adj.)

                           _____ (adv.)

hungry (adj.), p. 168   _____ (n.)   _____ (adv.)

Summarizing

Exercise 1. Read the following groups of sentences. Put the number 1 next to the event that happened first, 2 next to the second, and 3 next to the third. Notice that the verbs are in present tense.

1. ___ Alice and Isaac run away.

   ___ Dana takes care of Alice.

   ___ Rufus buys Alice.

2. ___ Alice sleeps in the attic with Dana.

   ___ Alice sleeps in Rufus's bed.

   ___ Alice sleeps in the trundle bed.

3. ___ Tom and Rufus find Dana.

   ___ Dana runs away.

   ___ Dana discovers that Rufus hadn't mailed her letters.

4. ___ Kevin arrives at the plantation.

   ___ Tom writes a letter to Kevin.

   ___ Kevin writes a letter to Tom.

5. ___ Kevin and Dana say good-bye to Alice.

   ___ Kevin arrives at the plantation.

   ___ Rufus tries to shoot Dana.

Exercise 2. Choose one of the following sections of the novel to summarize. Use present tense verbs in your summary.

1. Pages 154 to 160 (section 10)
2. Pages 168 to 174 (section 12)
3. Pages 181 through 188 (section 16)

Response Journals

Exercise 1. Focus on Alice and Sarah in this exercise. Read the following passages and find them in the novel. After you have read the passage in context, respond to it by completing some of the sentences below it.

Passage 1. She hushed me with a sharp hiss. "You got to learn to watch what you say! Don't you know there's folks in this house who love to carry tales?" (Sarah, p. 150)

This shows that

I think

Passage 2. "He ever beat you?"
    "No! Of course not!"
    "My man used to. He'd tell me I was the only one he cared about. Then, next thing I knew, he'd say I was looking at some other man, and he'd go to hittin'."
    "Carrie's father?"
    "No . . . my oldest boy's father. Miss Hannah, her father. He always said he'd free me in his will, but he didn't. It was just another lie." (Sarah, p. 151)

I guess

I wonder

Passage 3. "Good to marry a freeman. Mama always said I should."
    Mama was right, I thought. But I said nothing.
    "My father was a slave, and they sold him away from her. She said marrying a slave is almost bad as being a slave." (Alice, p. 156)

This passage shows

I don't understand

Passage 4. "You ought to be ashamed of yourself, whining and crying after some poor white trash of a man, black as you are. You always try to act so white. White nigger, turning against your own people!" (Alice, p. 165)

I guess

I don't like

I wonder

Passage 5. She began to cry. "I ought to take a knife in there with me and cut his damn throat." She glared at me. "Now go tell him that! Tell him I'm talking 'bout killing him!" (Alice, p. 167)

I wonder

This passage shows

Passage 6. "I'm lying. I can't run again. I can't. You be hungry and cold and sick out there, and so tired you can't walk. Then they find you and set the dogs on you . . . My Lord, the dogs . . ." She was silent for a moment. "I'm going to him. He knew I would sooner or later. But he don't know how I wish I had the nerve to just kill him!" (Alice, p. 168)

I (don't) understand

This passage shows

Exercise 2. Write response journals for two passages from pages 148 through 188 (sections 8 through 16).

Topics for Discussion

Exercise 1. Below is a time line with some important dates in Rufus's life. Work with your classmates to match the descriptions on the right with the dates on the time line. Then answer the questions below.

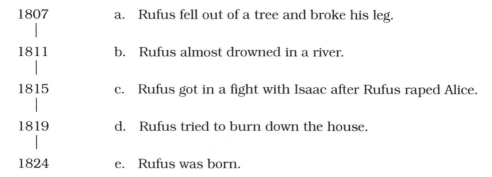

1807   a. Rufus fell out of a tree and broke his leg.

1811   b. Rufus almost drowned in a river.

1815   c. Rufus got in a fight with Isaac after Rufus raped Alice.

1819   d. Rufus tried to burn down the house.

1824   e. Rufus was born.

How old was Rufus when he

    tried to burn down the house? _____

    almost drowned in a river? _____

    fell out of a tree and broke his leg? _____

    got in a fight with Isaac? _____

Exercise 2. Using the Venn diagram on page 63, work with your classmates to place the descriptions about Kevin and Dana and Rufus and Alice in the diagram.

a. He loves her.
b. She loves him.
c. They are married.
d. They are an interracial couple.
e. She was married to someone else.
f. He is 12 years older than she is.
g. They are about the same age.
h. They knew each other when they were children.
i. They met at work.

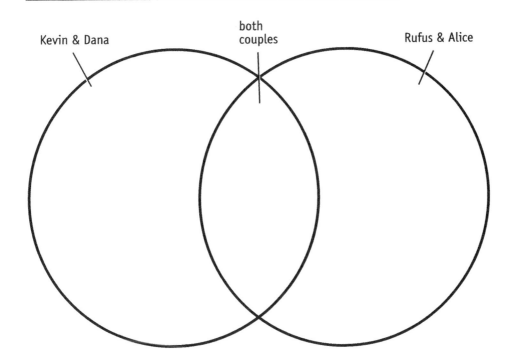

Kevin & Dana   both couples   Rufus & Alice

Composition

Exercise 1. Point-of-view writing. Use the information from the time line above to write several entries in Rufus's diary. Write about the times Dana came to save him. Remember that in order to do a point-of-view writing, you have to suspend disbelief and imagine that Rufus could write when he was four years old.

The first entry is done for you.

> June 20, 1811. Today I went swimming in the river and I almost drowned. I was walking along the river bottom when all of a sudden I fell into a hole and couldn't stand up anymore. When I closed my eyes, I could see a woman in a room with lots of books. Then the next thing I knew, that woman, dressed like a man, was carrying me out of the river and Mama was holding me. I don't know who that strange woman was.

Write diary entries for these dates.

September 15, 1815
April 30, 1819
August 29, 1824

Exercise 2. Read the following letter and decide who wrote it.

> Dear Kevin:
>
> Your woman, Dana, is back here at the plantation. I think you should come for her. She wrote you two letters, but my son didn't mail them. You need to get her soon because she ran away last night. We found her, but we had to whip her when we brought her back. I think she might run again, and I can't be responsible for what happens to her then. Please come soon.
>
> Yours truly,
>
> _____

Exercise 3. Point-of-view writing. Imagine that you are Alice. Write a letter to Isaac in Mississippi. Tell him everything that has happened to you since you were separated.

Beyond the Novel

Read these descriptions of African American abolitionists and complete the exercises below.

Frederick Douglass

Frederick Douglass was an orator and writer who became one of the most important abolitionists of the nineteenth century. He was born Frederick Augustus Washington Bailey near Easton, Maryland, in 1817. His father was a white man, and his mother was a slave. He never knew his father and was separated from his mother and raised by her parents. When he was eight years old he was sent to a new master, whose wife taught him to read. Later he worked in a shipyard in Baltimore and escaped by using the papers of a free black man. In 1838, he settled in Massachusetts and changed his name to Douglass.

In 1841, Frederick Douglass impressed the Massachusetts Antislavery Society with a speech about his experiences as a slave, and they hired him to speak for them. After that he joined other antislavery protests. Since he was eloquent and apparently well educated, some people doubted that he had been a slave. He told the world his story in his autobiography, *Narrative of the Life of Frederick Douglass,* in 1845. With the publication of the details of his life, Douglass feared that he might be captured and returned

This photograph shows Frederick Douglass, abolitionist, orator, and
writer. (Courtesy of the Library of Congress.)

to slavery, and so he moved to England where he continued to speak
against slavery. Some friends in England raised money to buy his freedom,
which allowed him to return to the United States. He returned in 1847 and
started an antislavery newspaper, *The North Star,* in Rochester, New York.
His home in New York was a station on the Underground Railroad. During
the Civil War, Frederick Douglass conferred with President Lincoln and
recruited African Americans to fight for the Union Army. After the Civil War,
Douglass held several positions in the U.S. government and worked for the
passage of the Fifteenth Amendment to the Constitution that gave black
men the right to vote in 1870. (Women of all races were not permitted to
vote until 1920 in the United States.) Douglass continued to work for the
rights of blacks and women until his death in 1895.

Harriet Tubman

Harriet Tubman was an escaped slave who became one of the most important figures in the Underground Railroad. She was born Harriet Ross on a plantation near Cambridge, Maryland, in 1820. Both of her parents were slaves. When she was 7 years old she began to do housework and care for white children. Later, she became a field hand, and by the time she was 19 years old she was as strong as the men she worked with. When she was 13, she was punished by a white master who hit her on the head. Although she recovered from her injury, for the rest of her life she fell asleep suddenly several times a day.

In 1844, Harriet married a free black man, John Tubman. She left him in 1849 and traveled north on the Underground Railroad because she was afraid of being sold farther South. Harriet Tubman worked as a maid in Philadelphia and saved money to return to Maryland to help more slaves escape. In 1850, she made her first journey to lead slaves out. After 19 trips, Harriet Tubman had helped about 300 slaves escape, including her parents and many of her 10 brothers and sisters.

Tubman insisted on strict discipline on the Underground Railroad. She carried a gun and threatened to kill anyone who became scared and wanted to turn back. And while slaveholders tried to capture her and the slaves she helped, not one was ever caught and returned to slavery.

Harriet Tubman served as a nurse and cook for the Union Army in the Civil War and after the war settled in Auburn, New York, where she established a home for elderly and needy blacks.

Sojourner Truth

Sojourner Truth was an abolitionist, evangelist, and orator who spoke out against slavery in the nineteenth century. She was born Isabella Baumfree around 1797 in New York State. She later took the name Isabella Van Wagener, after her last master. She was freed in 1827 when slavery was banned in New York.

In 1843, Isabella claimed to have been told by God to go out and preach, and so she changed her name to Sojourner Truth. She chose that name to symbolize her mission, which was to tell the people the truth in a series of "sojourns" or short stays. She progressed from evangelical messages to preaching against slavery and for women's rights.

During the Civil War, Sojourner Truth met with Abraham Lincoln in the White House. After that, she stayed in Washington, D.C., to help improve the living conditions of blacks. She also helped to settle freed slaves and tried to persuade the government to give lands in the undeveloped West to blacks.

Exercise 1. Decide if these phrases are about Frederick Douglass, Harriet Tubman, or Sojourner Truth. Write the initials F.D. for Frederick Douglass, H.T. for Harriet Tubman, and S.T. for Sojourner Truth. You may write one, two, or three sets of initials after each phrase.

1. was born a slave _____

2. escaped from the South to the North _____

3. returned to the South to help other slaves escape _____

4. was born in Maryland _____

5. was born in New York _____

6. took her husband's last name _____

7. took her master's last name _____

8. invented a new name _____

9. gave antislavery speeches _____

10. met Abraham Lincoln _____

11. lived in New York _____

12. lived in Massachusetts _____

13. participated in the Civil War _____

14. lived outside the United States _____

15. purchased his freedom _____

Exercise 2. Tell in what order the following events happened. Put the number 1 before the first event, 2 before the second, and 3 before the third.

1. __ Frederick Douglass was born.

    __ Harriet Tubman was born.

    __ Sojourner Truth was born.

2. __ Frederick Douglass settled in Massachusetts.

    __ Harriet Tubman escaped to the North.

    __ Sojourner Truth received her freedom.

3. __ Frederick Douglass wrote his autobiography.

__ Harriet Tubman made her first journey to free slaves.

__ Sojourner Truth began to use her new name.

Options

Activity 1. Complete this puzzle by filling in names and words. Then, copy the circled letters in order to complete the phrase below.

Family Ties

Rufus's mother is __ Ⓞ __ __ __ __ __ __ .

Jude is Carrie's __ __ Ⓞ __ .

Rufus is Tom's __ Ⓞ __ .

Carrie's husband is __ __ __ __ Ⓞ .

Dana's husband is __ __ __ Ⓞ __ .

Rufus's father is Ⓞ __ __ .

Nigel's wife is __ __ __ __ Ⓞ __ .

Margaret is Rufus's __ Ⓞ __ __ __ __ .

Kevin's wife is __ __ Ⓞ __ .

Sarah's daughter is __ __ __ __ Ⓞ __ .

Carrie's mother is Ⓞ __ __ __ __ .

Margaret's husband is Ⓞ __ __ .

Tom's son is __ __ __ __ Ⓞ .

Fill in with the circled letters.

Frederick Douglass, Harriet Tubman, and Sojourner Truth were

__ __ __ __ __ __ __ __ __ __ __ __ __ .

Activity 2. Role play. Work with a small group to role-play a scene from this section of the novel. First, write a script for your scene. You may have to invent some dialogue that does not appear in the novel. Then role-play the scene for the class. You may choose any scene with any number of characters that you wish. Here are some ideas.

1. Alice and Dana are in the kitchen, preparing dinner, while Sarah helps to deliver Carrie's baby. Alice regains her memory in this scene.
2. Alice, Tess, and Carrie confront Liza after Liza told Tom that Dana had run away.
3. Tom and Rufus talk after Tom discovered that Rufus hadn't mailed Dana's letters to Kevin.
4. Kevin, Dana, and Rufus argue while Kevin and Dana try to leave the plantation together.

Activity 3. Library work. Check out a biography or autobiography of Frederick Douglass, Harriet Tubman, or Sojourner Truth from your public library. The children's or young adults' sections of the library are good places to find easy-to-read biographies.

Unit Five

Looking Ahead

This unit covers pages 189 to 224, or about two-thirds of the chapter "The Storm" (sections 1 through 8). The section begins with Dana and Kevin arriving home safely. Then after less than a day at home, Dana is called again to Rufus.

Freewriting

Choose one of the following topics and write for about 15 minutes.

1. When Dana is called to Rufus in "The Storm," it is because Rufus is sick. Write about a time when you were very sick. What illness did you have? How did you feel? Who took care of you? Were you at home or in the hospital?

2. Margaret returns in this section, and she has changed a lot. Write about someone you know who has changed. How was the person before the change? How was the person after the change? Write about what caused the change if you know.

3. When Kevin returns home after five years in the past, he is confused and disoriented. Many things in his house, from the stove to the electric pencil sharpener, seem odd to Kevin. Remember the time when you first came to the United States or went to another country. What things did you find odd or unusual compared with what you were used to?

Test Yourself

Quiz 1. Pages 189 through 205 (sections 1 through 3). Authors support generalizations with examples. Read the generalizations on page 71 and circle the letters of all of the examples that appear in the novel.

1. Kevin told Dana about the experiences that he had while he was stranded in the past.

   a. He saw a woman die from a beating during childbirth.

   b. He almost bought a farm in Maine.

   c. He bought some slaves and sold them.

   d. He helped slaves escape by hiding them during the day.

2. Kevin acted out angrily when he realized that he didn't feel comfortable at home.

   a. He hit Dana.

   b. He banged his fist on his typewriter.

   c. He knocked his pencils and pencil sharpener off his desk.

   d. He left the house to take a long walk.

3. Dana repacked her denim bag.

   a. She put in a bottle of antiseptic.

   b. She packed a large bottle of Excedrin.

   c. She put in a good book to read on the plantation.

   d. She decided to take an old pocketknife.

4. Dana heard some news stories on the radio.

   a. Men landed on the moon for the first time.

   b. There was a war in Lebanon.

   c. Ronald Reagan was president.

   d. There were race riots in South Africa.

5. Rufus was sick.

   a. He was shaking violently while Nigel tried to keep him wrapped up.

   b. His eyes were red, and they hurt when he tried to look around.

   c. His hands hurt, and he couldn't hold a pencil.

   d. His head and his leg hurt.

Quiz 2. Pages 197 to 209 (sections 2 through 4). True or false?

__ 1. Dana found Rufus lying face up in a puddle.

__ 2. Dana asked Nigel to help her get Rufus into the house.

__ 3. Dana met Tom just inside the house.

__ 4. Tom wanted Dana to change because her clothes were wet.

__ 5. Tom wanted to talk to Dana in the library.

__ 6. Tom exclaimed that it had been six months since he'd last seen Dana.

__ 7. Tom and Dana had a friendly chat.

__ 8. Tom told Dana to take care of Rufus.

__ 9. Dana realized that ague is another name for malaria.

__ 10. Dana tried to explain to Nigel that mosquitoes carry malaria.

__ 11. Rufus and Dana decided that Rufus probably didn't have malaria (ague).

__ 12. Tom decided to send for the doctor.

__ 13. Sarah looked the same as usual.

__ 14. Sarah made some tea for Rufus, and Dana gave him some aspirins dissolved in water.

__ 15. Rufus was sick for six days and nights with constant pain and fever.

__ 16. Dana discovered that Hagar had been born.

__ 17. Alice said that her babies look more like her than like Rufus.

__ 18. Tom died of a heart attack.

Quiz 3. Pages 209 to 217 (sections 5 and 6). Complete the following sentences with information from the story.

1. Carrie and Nigel had _____ sons.

2. Alice's children died because _____.

3.   Rufus decided to punish Dana because _____

_____.

4.   To punish Dana, Rufus made her _____.

5.   In the cornfield, Dana had to _____.

6.   When Dana couldn't do the work, Evan Fowler _____

_____.

7.   Finally, Dana stumbled, fell, and _____.

8.   Rufus came to the cornfield to _____.

9.   When Dana tried to leave Rufus's room, he told her _____

_____.

10.   Dana reminded Rufus that she'd saved his life several times and

told him that _____.

11.   Rufus explained that he'd sent Dana to the field because _____

_____.

12.   Rufus told Dana that Margaret was coming home and that he

wanted _____.

13.   Dana realized that Margaret was addicted to _____.

14.   Dana discovered that Alice is going to have another baby. She hopes

that this baby will be _____.

**Quiz 4. Pages 217 to 224 (sections 7 and 8). Find two or more examples in
the story for each of the following questions.**

1.   How was Margaret different?

_____

_____

2.   What did Margaret want Dana to do for her?

_____

_____

3. What did Dana learn while she was taking care of Margaret?

_____

_____

4. Why did Dana like working for Margaret?

_____

_____

5. What did the slave coffle look like?

_____

_____

6. What did Carrie tell Dana after Tess was sold?

_____

_____

Vocabulary

For this section of the novel, add 10 words to your vocabulary log. Remember, for each word, you should have the following information.

    word (part of speech)
    other forms
    definition
    sentence copied from the novel

Don't forget to choose the one best definition of the word as it is used in the sentence that you copy.

Exercise 1. Word forms. Circle the correct word form in each sentence.

1. When Dana and Kevin got home, Kevin seemed (confused/confusion) about some of the modern conveniences in their house.

2. Kevin was (anger/angry) because he didn't feel comfortable in his own house.

3. When Dana found Rufus, he was (unconscious/unconsciously).

4. Tom told Dana to continue to (helpful/help) Rufus.

5. Rufus was (suffer/suffering) from an unknown illness.

6. Alice had two babies who (death/died).

7. Rufus (punishment/punished) Dana after Tom died.

8. Rufus (threatened/threat) to send Dana back to the fields.

9. Margaret was (addiction/addicted) to laudanum.

10. Margaret was (kinder/kindly) than she used to be.

Exercise 2. Choosing definitions. Find each of the following words in the novel. After you understand the context in which the word is used, circle the letter of the best definition.

1. Page 189. I couldn't have been <u>unconscious</u> for more than a minute.

   a. unconscious (adj.): knocked out, as in a deep sleep

   b. unconscious (adj.): involuntary, without thinking

2. Page 190. I found him <u>fiddling</u> with the stove, turning the burners on, staring into the blue flame, turning them off, opening the oven, peering in.

   a. fiddle (v.): to play a violin

   b. fiddle (v.): to move something with one's fingers without a purpose

3. Page 192. I went to him with <u>relief</u> that surprised me.

   a. relief (n.): the lessening of a concern or worry

   b. relief (n.): assistance given in time of trouble

4. Page 194. I had tried and tried and only <u>managed</u> to fill my waste-basket.

   a. manage (v.): to succeed at doing something

   b. manage (v.): to direct or administer a business

5. Page 194. He <u>stalked</u> out of the room before I could finish.

    a. stalk (v.): to follow something before attacking it

    b. stalk (v.): to walk in a stiff and angry way

Summarizing

Exercise 1. Read the following summary of pages 198 through 201 (section 2). There are several mistakes in the summary. Change words to correct the mistakes. Notice that the summary is written in present tense.

Dana is called again to Rufus and finds herself in the middle of a downpour. At first she doesn't see Rufus, but then she sees that he is face down in a snowdrift. She drags him away from the puddle and realizes that he is dead. She can't carry him to the house, so she goes to get Luke. Nigel is surprised to see her. After she and Nigel get Rufus into the house, they meet Sarah. Tom tells Dana to change her shoes and come to talk to him in the cookhouse. In the library, Tom tells Dana that she's been away for 16 years, and he can't understand why she still has the scab on her face from where he kicked her. They argue, and Dana notices that Tom seems strong and healthy. Tom tells Dana that she has to take care of Margaret.

Exercise 2. When you summarize dialogue, you write in reported speech. To change commands to reported speech, use "to" and change pronoun references. Fill in the blanks in the following to change direct quotations to reported speech. The first one has been done for you.

1. Page 195. "Leave me alone for a while, Dana," he said softly.

    Kevin asks Dana __to__ leave __him__ alone for a while.

2. Page 197. "Kevin, go get my bag."

    Dana tells Kevin _____ go get _____ bag.

3. Page 209. "Send Nigel to me," he whispered.

   Rufus orders Dana _____ send Nigel to _____.

4. Page 211. "Now do what the others do," he said. "Chop close to the ground. Chop hard!"

   Fowler tells _____ _____ do what the others do. He instructs her

   _____ chop close to the ground and _____ chop hard.

5. Page 212. I met the woman who had been working toward me and she whispered, "Slow down! Take a lick or two if you have to."

   The woman advises _____ _____ slow down. She urges her

   _____ take a lick or two if _____ has to.

6. Page 213. "Don't do anything stupid, Dana."

   Rufus warns _____ not _____ do anything stupid.

7. Page 214. "Don't you ever walk away from me again!" he said.

   Rufus orders Dana _____ never walk away from _____ again.

8. Page 217. "Go read a book or something. Don't do any more work today."

   Rufus permits Dana _____ go read a book or something. He

   instructs _____ not _____ do any more work that day.

9. Page 218. "Read the Bible to me," she said.

   Margaret asks Dana _____ read the Bible to _____.

10. Page 222. "Dana!" Rufus's voice from near the steps where he was talking with the other white man. "You get away from here. Go inside."

    Rufus is talking with the other white man near the steps, and he

    orders _____ _____ get away from there and tells _____ _____

    go inside.

Exercise 3. Choose one of the following sections of the novel to summarize.

1.   Pages 202 to 209
2.   Pages 209 to 213
3.   Pages 217 to 224 (sections 7 and 8)

Response Journals

Exercise 1. Read the following passages and find each one in the novel. After you have read the passage in context, respond to it by completing the sentences below each one.

Passage 1. I could recall walking along the narrow dirt road that ran past the Weylin house and seeing the house, shadowy in twilight, boxy and familiar, yellow light showing from some of the windows— Weylin was surprisingly extravagant with his candles and oil. I had heard that other people were not. I could recall feeling relief at seeing the house, feeling that I had come home. (p. 190)

I wonder

I think

Passage 2. With a sudden slash of his hand, he knocked both the sharpener and the cup of pencils from his desk. The pencils scattered and the cup broke. The sharpener bounced hard on the bare floor, just missing the rug. I unplugged it quickly. (p. 194)

I feel

This shows that

Passage 3. I made myself slow down. It wasn't hard. I didn't think my shoulders could have hurt much worse if they'd been broken. Sweat ran down into my eyes and my hands were beginning to blister. My back hurt from the blows I'd taken as well as from sore muscles. After a while, it was more painful for me to push myself than it was for me to let Fowler hit me. After a while, I was so tired, I didn't care either way. Pain was pain. After a while, I just wanted to lie down between the rows and not get up again. (p. 212)

I don't understand

This seems

Passage 4. Nigel carried her up to her room. She could walk a little, but she couldn't manage the stairs. Sometime later, she wanted to see Nigel's children. She was sugary sweet with them. (p. 218)

I'm surprised

I remember

Exercise 2. Write response journals for two passages from pages 189 to 224 (sections 1 through 8).

Topics for Discussion

Exercise 1. Relationships. Look at the following groups of words and names. Circle the item that you think doesn't belong with the others. Tell why you circled that item. There are no wrong answers as long as you can defend your choice.

1.	Easton	Baltimore	Altadena
2.	Rufus	Kevin	Tom
3.	Isaac	Luke	Nigel
4.	the cookhouse	the attic	the library
5.	Carrie	Dana	Alice

Exercise 2. Point-of-view quotations. Study each invented quotation below and tell which character you think might say that. Remember the whole novel and not just "The Storm."

1. "I was beating Dana one day after I caught her teaching Nigel to read, and she vanished right before my eyes!" _____

2. "Carrie was the only child that I got to keep." _____

3. "I traveled north after Dana left me in the past." _____

4. "I'm happy as long as I have my laudanum." _____

5. "They sold me to a trader heading to Mississippi after they cut off my ears." _____

Exercise 3. Who am I? Write quotations that one or more of these characters might say. Then read your quotations to your classmates. They will try to guess which character might say that.

Rufus	Dana	Alice	Luke	Nigel
Liza	Joe	Evan Fowler	Alice's mother	Carrie

_____

_____

_____

_____

_____

_____

_____

_____

_____

_____

_____

_____

_____

_____

_____

_____

_____

_____

_____

_____

Exercise 4. Kevin was quite confused when he returned to 1976. What if something went wrong in Kevin's time travel and he returned to this year instead? Work with your classmates to fill in the following chart.

	In 1976	*Today*
in the kitchen	electric range	
in the office	electric typewriter electric pencil sharpener	
in the living room	color television	
in the news	civil war in Lebanon	
in the sky	jet airplane	

Composition

Exercise 1. The world has changed a lot since 1976. Write a paper in which you tell what you think will surprise Kevin and Dana the most if they have the chance to time-travel to this year.

Exercise 2. Point-of-view writing. Imagine that you are Kevin. Write a letter to your friend the psychiatrist. Tell him about what has been happening to you and Dana lately.

Beyond the Novel

Kevin mentions Denmark Vesey. Read about Vesey and two other men who led uprisings against slavery, and then complete the exercises below.

Denmark Vesey (pronounced VEE zee) was born into slavery around 1767. He was a slave until he bought his freedom with money that he won in a street lottery. After he had his freedom, he worked as a carpenter in Charleston, South Carolina, where there were many free blacks as well as slaves. In Charleston, he plotted the largest slave revolt in American history. He organized as many as 9,000 free blacks and slaves and planned to have them attack several cities in South Carolina. The revolt was never carried out. Some white slaveholders found out about the plan, and in 1822 they hanged Vesey and 35 of his followers. After the failed revolt, South Carolina passed new laws restricting education, movement, and occupations of free blacks and slaves.

Nat Turner was born into slavery on October 2, 1800, on a plantation in Virginia. There he was allowed to learn to read and write. In 1831, Turner believed that a solar eclipse signaled that it was time to revolt, and so he planned the most famous slave revolt in American history. Turner and a small group of slaves killed about 60 whites in Virginia before they were captured and hanged by the Virginia militia. After the revolt, another 100 slaves were killed by angry whites. After Turner's revolt, Virginia passed laws prohibiting slaves from being educated, from moving freely, and from assembling in groups.

John Brown was born into a family of white abolitionists on May 9, 1800. He lived in various states throughout the North, including Connecticut, Ohio, Massachusetts, and Pennsylvania. His home in Pennsylvania was a station on the Underground Railroad. After working in the abolition movement for many years, Brown decided that violence was the only way to end slavery. In 1859, he led a group of 16 whites and 5 blacks in an attack on an arsenal in Harpers Ferry, West Virginia, to steal weapons. Brown and his followers took 60 hostages but finally surrendered. He was hanged later in 1859. While Brown's raid on the arsenal was unsuccessful, it helped bring on the start of the Civil War.

Exercise 1. Decide if these phrases are about Denmark Vesey, Nat Turner, or John Brown. Write the initials D.V. for Denmark Vesey, N.T. for Nat Turner, and J.B. for John Brown. You may write one, two, or three sets of initials after each phrase.

1.   was born a slave _____

2.   lived in the North _____

3.   lived in the South _____

4.   plotted the largest slave revolt _____

5.   plotted the most famous slave revolt _____

6.   used only blacks in his revolt _____

7.   led a group of blacks and whites _____

8.   revolt led to stricter laws governing blacks _____

9.   participated in the Underground Railroad _____

10. was hanged _____

Exercise 2. Fill in the following time line with information about Denmark Vesey, Nat Turner, and John Brown.

```
        1767          _____
          |
May 9, 1800           _____
          |
October 2, 1800       _____
          |
        1822          _____
          |
        1831          _____
          |
        1859          _____
```

Read the story of Peg Leg Joe and study the song that follows.

While Denmark Vesey, Nat Turner, and John Brown were plotting a violent end to slavery, the Underground Railroad continued to operate, escorting slaves to the North and to freedom. You read about the most famous conductor on the Underground Railroad, Harriet Tubman. Here is a story about another, less famous conductor.

Peg Leg Joe was a white man who had been a sailor. In his sailor days, he lost his right leg and replaced it with a peg. Then he became a handyman. He traveled from plantation to plantation across the South, doing odd jobs for the owners. His real work, however, was not fixing things on plantations; it was helping slaves escape.

Peg Leg Joe got to know the slaves on all the plantations where he worked, and he taught the slaves a song, "Follow the Drinkin' Gourd." The slave owners didn't think much of the song that Joe taught the slaves, but in the song were directions for escaping to the North. The Drinking Gourd in the title of the song refers to the constellation called the Big Dipper or Ursa Major, which points to the North Star. Slaves used the North Star to direct them, as they did not have compasses and could not follow roads for fear of being seen.

Study the song to find out what Peg Leg Joe taught the slaves. First, "when the sun comes back and the first quail calls" told the slaves that the best time to travel is in springtime. That way they could complete their journey in good weather. They could tell that it was springtime when the days got longer and the birds (such as quail) returned. Then, the "Old Man is a-waitin' for to carry you to freedom" told them that Peg Leg Joe would return to the North to carry them across the Ohio River.

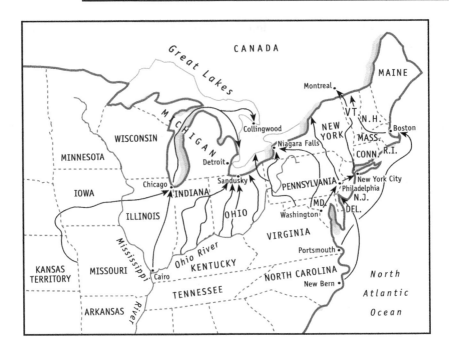

This map shows the set routes that escaping slaves followed through the North on the Underground Railroad after they made their way out of the South on their own.

"The river bank'll make a mighty good road" told the slaves to follow rivers on their escape. There, they could follow a path of "dead trees" that Peg Leg Joe had marked in charcoal with his symbol—a left foot and circle symbolizing a peg leg: "left foot, pegfoot, travelin' on."

The song held a bit of a geography lesson for the escaping slaves. The river that ended "'tween two hills" was the Tombigbee River. Then, the other "river on the other side" was the Tennessee River. After that, the slaves had only to cross the Ohio River and enter the free states. That was where Peg Leg Joe, "the Old Man" was waiting to ferry the slaves to freedom.

"Follow the Drinkin' Gourd"

Verse:

1. When the sun comes back and the first quail calls, Fol-low __ The Drink-in' Gourd. Then the

Old Man is a-wait-in' for to car-ry you to free-dom, Fol-low The Drink-in' Gourd.

Chorus:

Fol-low __ The Drink-in' Gourd, Fol-low__ The Drink-in' Gourd, For the

Old Man is a-wait-in' for to car-ry you to free-dom, Fol-low The Drink-in' Gourd. 2. Now the

2.
Now the river bank'll make a mighty good road; The dead trees'll show you the way.
And the left foot, pegfoot, travelin' on, Just you Follow The Drinkin' Gourd. *(Chorus)*

3.
Now the river ends 'tween two hills; Follow The Drinkin' Gourd.
And there's another river on the other side, Just you Follow The Drinkin' Gourd. *(Chorus)*

Options

Activity 1. Analogies. Analogies are like equations with words. Study this example.

Dana:California = Rufus:Maryland

Complete these equations with the most logical word or name.

1. Dana:black = Rufus: _____

2. Alice:Joe = Carrie: _____

3. Alice:Isaac = Dana: _____

4. Easton:Maryland = Altadena: _____

5. Tom:Rufus = Luke: _____

6. "The River":drown = "The Storm": _____

7. John Brown:Harpers Ferry = Denmark Vesey: _____

8. Tess:fields = Sarah: _____

9. Dana:pants = Alice: _____

10. Frederick Bailey:Frederick Douglass = Harriet Ross: _____

11. Tom:plantation owner = Kevin: _____

12. Sarah:Miss Hannah's father = Alice: _____

13. Dana:twentieth century = Rufus: _____

14. the Big Dipper:the Drinking Gourd = the Tennessee River:

    _____

15. Nat Turner:Virginia = Denmark Vesey: _____

Activity 2. Role play. Work with a small group to role-play a scene in which Peg Leg Joe arrives at a new plantation. First, write the script in which Peg Leg Joe explains his song to several slaves. Then role-play your scene for the class.

Activity 3. Library work. Go to your local library and look for information on Denmark Vesey, Nat Turner, or John Brown. Or check out a video or children's picture book that tells the story of Peg Leg Joe and the song "Follow the Drinkin' Gourd."

Unit Six

Looking Ahead

This unit covers pages 224 through 264, the end of the novel. This section of the novel is the last part of "The Storm," all of the chapter entitled "The Rope," and the "Epilogue." You may also want to go back and reread the "Prologue" at some point as you finish the novel.

At the end of "The Storm," Hagar is born. Alice considers running away, and Rufus angers Dana so much that she does something to herself that causes her to return home. She has 15 days at home with Kevin and then is called back to the past one final time.

Freewriting

Choose one of the following topics and write for 15 minutes.

1. At the end of "The Storm," Alice has two children: Joe, a little boy, and Hagar, an infant. Although the children's father is white, they will grow up to be slaves. Alice is thinking about taking the children and trying to escape to the North. Do you think she should try to run away? Why or why not?

2. Dana does something at the end of "The Storm" that causes her to go home. You remember that in order to travel back through time, Dana has to believe that her life is in danger. Write about several things that Dana might be able to do to cause her to travel home.

3. After Dana gets home, she will discuss with Kevin whether she should kill Rufus now that Hagar has been born. Write about whether Dana should kill Rufus. What are the advantages to killing him? What are the disadvantages?

4. While Dana is home with Kevin, she remarks that the experiences that they shared while they were in the past have brought them closer together. Write about some difficult experiences that you have had and tell who experienced them with you. Did the experiences bring you closer to the other person?

Test Yourself

Quiz 1. Pages 224 through 239 (sections 9 through 13 of "The Storm").
Circle the word or words that best complete the following statements.

1. The doctor told Rufus that he had had (dengue fever/smallpox).

2. Rufus suggested that if he dies, all the slaves will (go free/be sold).

3. Rufus asked Dana to (continue to take care of Margaret/help him with business matters).

4. Rufus allowed the slaves to have a party while they (husked the corn/chopped the wood).

5. A large man asked Dana to (marry him/dance with him) at the Christmas party.

6. Rufus was (happy/angry) that the slave was paying attention to Dana.

7. Alice convinced Rufus to have Dana teach Joe how to (ride a horse/read and write).

8. Alice wanted Rufus to (sell/free) Joe.

9. Rufus wanted Alice to (like/ignore) him.

10. Alice planned to run away and asked Dana to steal some (whiskey/laudanum) to keep the baby quiet.

11. Rufus told Dana and Alice that he planned to (free/sell) Joe, but he didn't show them any freedom papers.

12. Dana began to (teach/take care of) Nigel's sons and two other children.

13. Sam Jones, the man who had asked Dana to dance, asked her to (watch/teach) his younger brother and sister.

14. Rufus (killed/sold) Sam after he caught him talking to Dana.

15. Dana (shot herself/cut her wrists) in order to go home.

Quiz 2. Pages 240 through 264 ("The Rope" and "Epilogue"). Write a short answer for each of the following.

1. Why did Dana cut her wrists?

    _____

    _____

2. Who bandaged Dana's wrists?

    _____

    _____

3. What did Dana and Kevin discuss doing to Rufus now that Hagar had been born?

    _____

    _____

4. What problems would killing Rufus (or letting him die) cause? Why was Dana afraid that she might not get home?

    _____

    _____

5. Why was Dana called to the past again?

    _____

    _____

6. Where did Dana find Alice?

    _____

    _____

7. Why did Alice do it?

    _____

    _____

8. Where had Rufus been heading when Dana arrived?

    _____

    _____

9. What had Rufus really done with the children? Why?

10. What did Dana demand from Rufus?

11. What did Rufus get at the courthouse?

12. What dreams did Rufus tell Dana about?

13. Where did Rufus follow Dana?

14. What did Dana hold in her hand as they talked?

15. Where was Rufus's hand after Dana stabbed him?

16. Who discovered Rufus and Dana in the attic?

17. What was wrong with Dana's arm when she arrived home?

18. Where did Dana and Kevin go after her arm was well?

_____

_____

19. What did Nigel do to cover up Rufus's murder?

_____

_____

20. What happened to most of the slaves?

_____

_____

This photograph shows the Talbot County Historical Society in Easton, Maryland, today.

Quiz 3. Pages 224 through 264. Choose several of the following passages and prepare to interpret them for your classmates. The first one is done for you.

Page 225: Rufus leaned back and looked at me wearily. "Do you know what would happen to the people here if I died?"

I nodded.

Interpretation: Rufus is asking Dana if she realizes that all of the slaves will be sold if he dies, and she is telling him that she knows that.

Page 228. "Behold the woman," he said. And he looked from one to the other of us. "You really are only one woman. Did you know that?"

Interpretation:

Page 228. "We look alike if we can believe our own eyes!"

"I guess so. Anyway, all that means we're two halves of the same woman—at least in his crazy head."

Interpretation:

Page 229. Strangely, they seemed to like him, hold him in contempt, and fear him all at the same time.

Interpretation:

Page 230. "What would you do if I had found someone?" I asked. "Sell him," he said. His smile was still in place, but there was no longer any humor in it.

Interpretation:

Page 232. "I don't mean to spend my life here watching my children grow up as slaves and maybe get sold."

Interpretation:

Page 233. For the first and only time, I saw her smile at him—a real smile.

Interpretation:

Page 233. They called the baby Hagar. Rufus said it was the ugliest name he had ever heard, but it was Alice's choice, and he let it stand. I thought it was the most beautiful name I had ever heard.

Interpretation:

Page 234. "He'll never let any of us go," she said. "The more you give him, the more he wants." She paused, wiped her eyes, then added softly, "I got to go while I still can—before I turn into just what people call me."

Interpretation:

Page 242. "Then . . . it doesn't seem to me that you have such a difficult decision ahead of you."

Interpretation:

Page 243. With some kind of reverse symbolism, Rufus called me back on July 4.

Interpretation:

Vocabulary

For this section of the novel, add 10 words to your vocabulary log. Remember, for each word, you should have the following information.

word (part of speech)
other forms
definition
sentence copied from the novel

Don't forget to choose the one best definition of the word as it is used in the sentence that you copy.

Exercise 1. Word forms. Fill in each sentence with the correct word form.

1. silence   silent   silently

    a. Sometimes Dana sat _____ in Margaret's room.

    b. Margaret was often _____ after she took her laudanum.

    c. Dana appreciated the _____ in Margaret's room.

2. persuasion   persuade   persuasive

    a. Alice tried to _____ Rufus to free the children.

    b. Dana was often very _____ with Rufus.

    c. After a while, Dana's _____ worked.

3. patience   patient   patiently

    a. Alice said that Rufus was more _____ when Dana was around.

    b. Dana taught Joe very _____.

    c. Margaret seemed to have more _____ than she used to.

4. curiosity   curious   curiously

    a. Joe seemed to have a lot of _____.

    b. Joe was _____ about everything.

    c. Joe sat on Rufus's lap and studied the map _____.

5. anger   angry   angrily

    a. Sometimes Alice spoke _____ to Dana.

    b. Alice said that Rufus didn't get so _____ when Dana was there.

    c. Often slaves tried not to show their _____.

6. dangers   endanger   dangerous

   a. Alice could _____ the lives of her children by running away with them.

   b. Many whites thought that it was _____ to educate slaves.

   c. Alice said she understood about the _____ involved with running away.

7. caution   cautious   cautiously

   a. Some of the field slaves spoke _____ around Dana and Alice.

   b. Alice knew that she had to use great _____ in preparing to run away.

   c. The slaves were usually very _____ around the owners.

8. innocence   innocent   innocently

   a. Sam was _____, but Rufus sold him anyway.

   b. Dana tried to convince Rufus of Sam's _____.

   c. Sam spoke _____ to Dana.

9. desperation   desperate   desperately

   a. Dana acted _____ when she cut her wrists.

   b. Dana cut her wrists in _____.

   c. Dana was _____ when she cut her wrists.

10. differences   differ   different

    a. How do Dana and Alice _____?

    b. What are some of the _____ between Alice and Sarah?

    c. How are Rufus and Kevin _____?

Summarizing

Exercise 1. Read the following summary of pages 236 through 239 (section 13). There are several mistakes in the summary. Change words to correct the mistakes. Notice that the summary is written in past tense.

Dana started to teach some of the slave children to read and write. Some of Rufus's neighbors found out, and they thought it was a good idea. One day, a slave named Robert stopped Dana outside the cookhouse. He was the slave who had asked her to dance at the birthday party. Robert wanted Dana to teach his mother and father how to read and write. Dana told him to talk to her again. A few days later, Rufus whipped Sam. Dana was happy. She took too many sleeping pills and traveled back to the present.

Exercise 2. When you summarize dialogue, you write in reported speech. To change statements to reported speech, use "that" and change pronoun references. Add names where necessary. If you are using past tense, change present verbs to past and past verbs to past perfect. Fill in the blanks in the following to change direct quotations to reported speech. The first one has been done for you.

1. Page 224. "I'll send her back later, Mama. And Carrie'll be up to finish your bed in a minute."

    Rufus told Margaret ___that___ he ___would___ send Dana back later. Then he added that Carrie ___would___ be up to finish ___her___ bed soon.

2. Page 226. "I brought you down here to write a few letters for me, not fight with me."

    Rufus told Dana _____ _____ had brought _____ there to write a few letters for _____, not to fight with _____.

3. Page 228. "You know," she said, "you gentle him for me. He hardly hits me at all when you're here. And he never hits you."

    Alice told Dana _____ _____ gentled Rufus for _____. She

    added _____ he hardly _____ _____ at all when _____ was

    there. And she added that Rufus never _____ Dana.

4. Page 230. "One husband is enough for me," I said.

    Dana commented _____ one husband _____ enough for

    _____.

5. Page 232. "He wants me to like him," she said with heavy contempt.

    Alice told Dana _____ Rufus _____ _____ to like him.

6. Page 238. "Rufe, please! Listen, he came to ask me to teach his brother and sister to read. That's all!"

    Dana told Rufus _____ Sam _____ _____ to ask _____ to

    teach his brother and sister to read.

7. Page 242. "Then . . . it doesn't seem to me that you have such a difficult decision ahead of you."

    Kevin told Dana _____ it _____ seem to _____ that _____

    _____ such a difficult decision ahead of _____.

8. Pages 247–248. "I don't know what I'm doing here, Rufe. I never do until I find out what's wrong with you."

    Dana told Rufus _____ _____ _____ know what _____

    _____ doing there. She added that _____ never _____ until

    she _____ out what was wrong with _____.

9. Page 250. "I didn't want to even be close to her. When Marse Tom sold my babies, I just wanted to lay down and die. Seeing her like she was brought all that back."

    Sarah told Dana _____ _____ hadn't wanted to be close to

    Alice. She told her that when Tom _____ _____ _____ babies,

    _____had just wanted to lie down and die. She added _____

    seeing Alice like she was had brought all that back.

10. Page 264. "It's over," he said. "There's nothing you can do to change any of it now."

    Kevin told Dana _____ it _____ over. He explained to her

    _____ there _____ nothing _____ _____ do to change any

    of it then.

Exercise 3. Choose one of the following sections of the novel to summarize. Use past tense verbs.

1. Pages 224 to 228 (sections 9 and 10)
2. Pages 228 to 236 (sections 11 and 12)
3. Pages 247 to 251 (section 3)
4. Pages 257 through 261

Response Journals

Exercise 1. Read the following passages and find each one in the novel. After you have read the passage in context, respond to it by completing the sentences below each one.

Passage 1. To my surprise, her stony expression crumbled, and she began to cry. "He'll never let any of us go," she said. "The more you give him, the more he wants." She paused, wiped her eyes, then added softly, "I got to go while I still can—before I turn into just what people call me." (p. 234)

This passage shows

I think

Passage 2. I saw Sam beyond him being chained into line. There were people a few feet away from him crying loudly. Two women, a boy and a girl. His family.

"Rufe," I pleaded desperately, "don't do this. There's no need!"

He pushed me back toward the door and I struggled against him.

"Rufe, please! Listen, he came to ask me to teach his brother and sister to read. That's all!" (p. 238)

This passage shows

I feel

Passage 3. "Have you decided what you're going to do about Rufus?" he asked.

I shook my head. "You know, it's not only what will happen to the slaves that worries me . . . if I turn my back on him. It's what might happen to me." (page 246)

I think

I wonder

Passage 4. Sarah put down her cleaver and sat on the bench next to the table. "Oh Lord. Poor child. He finally killed her."

"I don't know," I said. I went over and sat beside her. "I think she did it to herself. Hung herself. I just took her down."

"He did it!" she hissed. "Even if he didn't put the rope on her, he drove her to it. He sold her babies!" (p. 249)

I agree/don't agree

I think

Passage 5. "You know, Dana," he said softly, "when you sent Alice to me that first time, and I saw how much she hated me, I thought, I'll fall asleep beside her and she'll kill me. She'll hit me with a candlestick. She'll set fire to the bed. She'll bring a knife up from the cookhouse . . .

"I thought all that, but I wasn't afraid. Because if she killed me, that would be that. Nothing else would matter. But if I lived, I would have her. And, by God, I had to have her." (p. 257)

This passage shows

I wonder

Exercise 2. Write response journals for two passages from pages 224 through 264.

Topics for Discussion

Exercise 1. Below is a Venn diagram. Work with your classmates to place the descriptions about Alice and Sarah in the diagram.

She was a slave.
She was born a slave.
She was born free.
She was married to a slave.
She lost her husband.
Her husband was sold.
Her husband was killed in an accident.
She had children who were fathered by a white man.
She believed that her children were sold.
She wanted her children to learn to read.
She was afraid of education.
She tried to run away.
She didn't like to think about running away.
She had the opportunity to kill her master.
Her master promised freedom to her or her children.

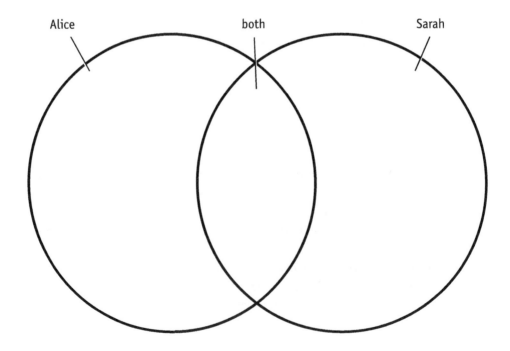

Alice   both   Sarah

Exercise 2. Now that you have finished the novel, choose one or more of the following questions to discuss with your classmates.

1. Reread the beginning of the "Prologue." Why do you think the author began the novel this way? Do you like the beginning?

2. Dana first travels to the past shortly after they move into a new house. Do you think the house has anything to do with her time travel? Do you think they should continue to live in that house?

3. How did you feel about Rufus while you were reading the novel? Why do you think the author introduced us to Rufus when he was a boy? Would you have felt differently about him if you had met him when he was already an adult?

4. How would the novel be different if Kevin were black?

5. What is the significance of the wall that Dana's arm is crushed into at the end of the novel?

6. Why did Dana and Kevin travel to Easton and Baltimore? Would you like to visit the places in Maryland where the novel took place?

7. Dana lost an arm as part of her experience. What else did she lose? What did she gain?

Composition

Topic 1. Write a short essay in which you compare and contrast Alice and Sarah. How are they similar? How are they different? You may want to analyze the causes of their similarities and differences.

Topic 2. Point-of-view writing. Write Alice's suicide note. In the note, she looks back over her life, and she tells why she feels she has no choice but to kill herself.

Beyond the Novel

Read the following description and study the time line. Then complete the exercises below.

At the end of the Civil War in 1865, nearly four million slaves were set free. They were generally unprepared to live on their own, since they were uneducated and had no property or money. Many freed slaves worked for the same people who had been their masters, picking cotton for very low wages.

For a short period after the Civil War, blacks enjoyed the right to vote and hold office. Soon, however, as southern whites regained strength after their defeat in the war, they began to enact laws that restricted the blacks' new freedoms. Some laws forbade blacks to own land or carry guns, and others imposed curfews or made it legal to jail a black who didn't have a job. And other laws mandated segregated schools and trains and made interracial marriage illegal. While the Fifteenth Amendment to the Constitution gave black men the right to vote in 1870, many states barred them from voting by charging a poll tax that they could not pay or giving them a literacy test that they could not pass. White men who could not read or afford the poll tax were permitted to vote under a "grandfather clause" that allowed men to vote whose direct ancestors had voted before January 1, 1867. In addition to laws restricting blacks, white supremacist organizations like the Ku Klux Klan kept blacks from voting, holding office, or enjoying other rights by threatening them with violence.

It was not until the middle of the twentieth century that the civil rights movement began. Here is a time line of events in the civil rights movement.

1954	The Supreme Court ruled that segregated schools were unconstitutional and ordered the integration of all public schools.
1955	Rosa Parks was arrested in Montgomery, Alabama, for refusing to move to the back of a segregated bus. Dr. Martin Luther King, Jr., who at the time was a young pastor at a Baptist church in Montgomery, organized a boycott of the bus company. The boycott lasted 381 days and ended with a Supreme Court decision that segregation of buses was illegal. The Montgomery bus boycott is generally considered to be the beginning of the nonviolent civil rights movement.
1957	President Dwight Eisenhower sent ten thousand National Guard troops to escort nine black children into the all-white Central High School in Little Rock, Arkansas. The school was eventually integrated.
1961	Groups of blacks and whites known as freedom riders traveled from the North to the South to force the integration of interstate buses. Riots broke out in Montgomery, Alabama, when the freedom riders arrived there.
1963	Approximately 250,000 people joined the March on Washington, D.C., to support the fight for civil rights. Dr. Martin Luther King, Jr., gave his moving "I Have a Dream" speech from the steps of the Lincoln Memorial.
1964	Dr. Martin Luther King, Jr., was awarded the Nobel Peace Prize for his work in the nonviolent civil rights movement.

1964	The Twenty-fourth Amendment to tho Constitution made it illegal to deny voting rights to anyone who has failed to pay a tax.
1964	The Civil Rights Act prohibited discrimination in employment, schools, or any other public place based on race, color, religion, or national origin. The bill created the Equal Employment Opportunity Commission.
1965	The Voting Rights Act made it illegal to ask voters to pass literacy tests before they could register to vote. In many areas, less than one-half of eligible voters were registered due to the literacy requirement.
1965	Dr. Martin Luther King, Jr., led a drive to help people register to vote in Selma, Alabama. They were violently attacked, and so they organized a five-day march from Selma to Montgomery to protest their treatment.
1968	Dr. Martin Luther King, Jr., was assassinated in Memphis, Tennessee. Massive demonstrations were held across the country, and several race riots developed in urban areas from the demonstrations. Military force was used to break up the riots.

Exercise 1. Could it have happened? If Dana was 26 in 1976, then she was born in 1950. Put a check next to each of the following that you think could have happened in her life.

__ Dana attended a segregated kindergarten class when she was four years old. After that, her school was integrated.

__ When Dana was two, her father was not permitted to vote because he did not have enough money to pay a poll tax.

__ Dana was one of the nine black children who were escorted into Central High School by National Guard troops.

__ As a young teenager, Dana attended the March on Washington and heard King's "I Have a Dream" speech.

__ Dana attended a segregated high school.

__ Dana voted in her first election in 1964, when the Twenty-fourth Amendment was added to the Constitution.

__ Dana saw riots in Los Angeles when she was 18 years old.

__ Dana met Dr. Martin Luther King, Jr., when she was 20 years old.

__ Dana had to take a literacy test in order to register to vote when she turned 21 in 1971.

__ Dana had to pay a poll tax before she could vote for Jimmy Carter in 1976.

Exercise 2. Put the following events in order. Write the number 1 next to the event that happened first, 2 next to the second, and 3 next to the third.

1. __ The Civil War ended.

   __ Blacks had many rights, including the right to vote.

   __ Whites began to restrict the rights of blacks again.

2. __ Martin Luther King, Jr., won the Nobel Peace Prize.

   __ Martin Luther King, Jr., led a voter registration drive in Selma.

   __ Martin Luther King, Jr., organized a bus boycott.

3. __ The Supreme Court integrated public schools.

   __ The Voting Rights Act eliminated literacy tests for voters.

   __ The Twenty-fourth Amendment eliminated poll taxes.

4. __ President Eisenhower ordered the integration of a high school in Little Rock.

   __ Rosa Parks was arrested.

   __ King gave his "I Have a Dream" speech.

Options

Activity 1. Character match. How many characters can you remember from the novel? Match the clauses on the right with those on the left to create character descriptions with relative clauses.

__ 1. Dana was the woman

__ 2. Rufus was the one

__ 3. Kevin was the man

__ 4. Alice was the slave

__ 5. Margaret was the one

__ 6. Tom was the man

__ 7. The patrollers were people

__ 8. Buz was the one

a. who helped Tom beat Dana after she ran away.

b. who owned Isaac.

c. who was married to Dana.

d. who would become Dana's ancestor.

e. who was married to Tom before he married Margaret.

f. who looked for runaway slaves.

g. who alerted Tom when Dana ran away.

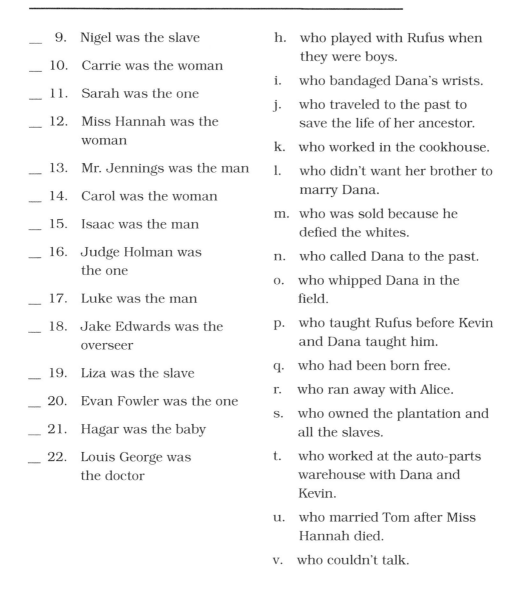

___ 9.   Nigel was the slave

___ 10.   Carrie was the woman

___ 11.   Sarah was the one

___ 12.   Miss Hannah was the
          woman

___ 13.   Mr. Jennings was the man

___ 14.   Carol was the woman

___ 15.   Isaac was the man

___ 16.   Judge Holman was
          the one

___ 17.   Luke was the man

___ 18.   Jake Edwards was the
          overseer

___ 19.   Liza was the slave

___ 20.   Evan Fowler was the one

___ 21.   Hagar was the baby

___ 22.   Louis George was
          the doctor

h.   who played with Rufus when
     they were boys.

i.   who bandaged Dana's wrists.

j.   who traveled to the past to
     save the life of her ancestor.

k.   who worked in the cookhouse.

l.   who didn't want her brother to
     marry Dana.

m.   who was sold because he
     defied the whites.

n.   who called Dana to the past.

o.   who whipped Dana in the
     field.

p.   who taught Rufus before Kevin
     and Dana taught him.

q.   who had been born free.

r.   who ran away with Alice.

s.   who owned the plantation and
     all the slaves.

t.   who worked at the auto-parts
     warehouse with Dana and
     Kevin.

u.   who married Tom after Miss
     Hannah died.

v.   who couldn't talk.

Activity 2. Library work. Go to your public library and borrow books or videos about the civil rights movement. Look for a book about Martin Luther King, Jr., in the children's or young adults' section of your library.

Activity 3. Role play. Role-play a scene in which Dana and Kevin make plans to visit Maryland after her arm heals. In the scene, one has to convince the other to go. Why should they go? Why shouldn't they go? Work in pairs. First, write a script for your scene. Then role-play it for your classmates.

Projects

1. Choose a scene in the novel that you especially liked and make a three-dimensional model of it. You may use a shoebox or other box or make your scene on a board. Use paper cutouts or clay, or dolls and other figures. Describe your scene to your classmates when you present your project.

2. Prepare some food mentioned in the novel and share it with your classmates. You may want to make corn bread, ham, fried chicken, or a peach cobbler.

3. Dress as a character from the novel and prepare a short speech telling who you are and the part you have in the novel.

4. Create a new book cover for the novel. Prepare a picture for the front cover and write a short synopsis for the back cover along with some opinions of the novel from some critics in your class. When you present your project to your class, tell them the significance of the picture that you chose.

5. Work with a partner. One partner will be a television interviewer, and the other will be a character from the novel. Interview the character about his or her role in the novel and how he or she felt about some of the other characters and action in the novel. Write up your dialogue and present it to the class.

6. Make a poster advertising a movie of *Kindred*. When you present your poster to your classmates, tell them which actors you have chosen for each part and why you chose them.

7. Write (but don't send) a letter to Octavia Butler. Tell her what you thought about the book and give her some ideas for another book with some of the same characters. Read your letter aloud to your classmates.

8. Go to your public library or local bookstore and look for some other novels by Octavia Butler. They may be shelved with science fiction. Bring the books to class and show them to your classmates.

9. Research Octavia Butler. You may find some information about her on the Internet or in newspaper and magazine articles. Present the information that you find to your classmates.

10. Learn some African American spirituals and teach them to your class. You may want to choose "Swing Low, Sweet Chariot" or "Rock-a My Soul."

Answer Key

Before You Begin

Summarizing

Exercise 1 (answers will vary)

Summary 1: Rufus; drowning

Summary 2: river; boy; him

Summary 3: river; noticed; drowning; swam; river; boy; mother; rifle; dizzy

Summary 4: Dana; river; boy; drowning; out; took; boy; mother; saving; Rufus; strange; father; rifle; heard; dizzy

Vocabulary Log

Exercise 1 (answers will vary)

line 9: (v.) to use great effort to do something

line 13: accidental (adj.), accidentally (adv.)

line 20: persistence (n.); persistent (adj.), persistently (adv.)

"Who then?" they persisted.

line 24: (n.)

no other forms (for this meaning)

responsibility for a mistake

Unit One

Test Yourself

Quiz 1: 1. F; 2. F; 3. T; 4. F; 5. F; 6. T; 7. T; 8. T; 9. F; 10. F; 11. T; 12. T; 13. F; 14. F; 15. F

Quiz 2: 1. nighttime; 2. still on the road; 3. free papers; 4. white; 5. whipped/knocked unconscious; 6. father; 7. New York; 8. a patroller; 9. returned to her home; 10. hours/minutes

Quiz 3 (answers will vary): 1. clothes, shoes, a knife; 2. whites who look for runaway slaves; 3. a certificate of freedom to forge; 4. believes that her life is in danger; 5. believes that he is going to die

Vocabulary

Exercise 1: 1. b; 2. b; 3. a; 4. b; 5. b

Summarizing

Exercise 1 (answers will vary): walks; finds; runs; feels; notices; sees; stays; ask; whip; punch

Response Journals
Exercise 1: S; R; R; S

Topics for Discussion
Possible problems (solutions) (answers will vary):

Kevin doesn't believe her. (take a camera with her/bring something back from the past/take him with her); She can't control when she goes to the past. (tie herself to something big/move to another house); She can't come home from the past when she wants to. (put herself in danger/try to kill herself); She has to keep Rufus alive until Hagar is born. (bring him to the present/take medicine to keep him healthy); When she is in the past, she is a black woman in slave times. (bring a certificate of freedom/wear a wig and paint her face so she looks white/go north); She has to make sure Alice and Rufus get together so that Hagar can be born. (stay in the past until this happens/talk to Alice); She looks like a man in the past. (wear old-fashioned clothes/pretend that she is a man).

Beyond the Novel
Exercise 1: 1. 213; 2. 132; 3. 213; 4. 231; 5. 132
Exercise 2: 1. no; 2. no; 3. 7; 4. 24; 5. because California isn't a state yet
Exercise 3 (answers will vary)

Options
Crossword
Across: 2. Hagar; 4. Kevin; 6. Maryland; 7. river; 8. time; 9. Rufus; 13. patroller; 14. town; 15. police
Down: 1. dizzy; 3. accident; 5. California; 10. ancestor; 11. arm; 12. Alice

Unit Two

Test Yourself
Quiz 1 (answers will vary): 1. auto-parts warehouse; 2. white; 3. are dead; 4. forgeable free papers; 5. held on to her; 6. out of a tree; 7. wife; 8. the future and California; 9. holding on to Dana

Quiz 2 (answers will vary): 1. father; 2. stay; 3. New York; 4. rough; 5. Dana; 6. talk; 7. hated; 8. black, white

Quiz 3 (answers will vary): 1. They were sold. 2. She is angry. 3. He held on to her because he wanted to go with her. 4. They realized that Kevin couldn't get back without Dana. 5. Tom asked Kevin to teach Rufus. 6. Kevin said that he was doing research for a book and that Dana was his slave. 7. Margaret doesn't like Dana; she's interested in Kevin (according to Sarah on p. 95). 8. Dana began to read to Rufus. 9. He was sold. 10. He asked her to teach Rufus. 11. It was Margaret's idea to sell Sarah's children. 12. Luke's advice was to say "yes, sir" to the whites and then do what you want to do. 13. Dana began to teach Nigel how to read. 14. The children were pretending to auction slaves. 15. Tom whipped Dana.

Vocabulary

Exercise 1: 1. i; 2. l; 3. c; 4. j; 5. e; 6. k; 7. a; 8. g; 9. b; 10. h; 11. d; 12. f

Summarizing

Exercise 1 (answers will vary): told; walked; noticed; realized; took; saw; gave; said; explained; gave; asked; said

Response Journals

Exercise 1: S; S; R; R

Topics for Discussion

Exercise 1. Mind map (answers will vary): general ideas (examples): poor living conditions (slept in attic, cabins with dirt floors); poor food (ate leftovers, corn-meal mush); couldn't move freely (Alice's father didn't have a pass); couldn't learn to read or write (Dana taught Nigel secretly; Dana was whipped for reading in the cookhouse); families were separated (Alice's father was sold; Sarah's children were sold); marriage was restricted (interracial marriage not allowed; Rufus was surprised that Kevin and Dana were married); they were beaten or whipped (Alice's father; Dana)

Exercise 2. Venn diagram: Slaves: They lived in cabins with dirt floors; They could not learn how to read or write; They could not leave the plantation without a pass. Both: They lived and worked on plantations, far from towns or cities; They didn't have good medical care; They didn't have electricity; Their food might be contaminated; They caught diseases from flies and mosquitoes; They used outdoor toilets; They used open fires for heating and cooking; They didn't have running water in their houses; They didn't bathe or wash clothes frequently. Slaveholders: They lived in fear that slaves would revolt; Mail delivery was slow and unreliable; Only boys went to school.

Beyond the Novel

Exercise 1: 1. 231; 2. 312; 3. 312

Exercise 2: 1. T; 2. F; 3. F; 4. T; 5. F; 6. F; 7. T; 8. T

Exercise 3: 1. F; 2. T; 3. F; 4. F; 5. T; 6. F; 7. T; 8. T

Options

Activity 1: 1. f; 2. a; 3. d; 4. h; 5. i; 6. j; 7. e; 8. c; 9. g; 10. b

Unit Three

Test Yourself

Quiz 1: 1. didn't like; 2. love; 3. didn't approve of; 4. have lighter skin; 5. someone like him; 6. Las Vegas

Quiz 2 (answers will vary): 1. in her bathroom at home; 2. still in the past; 3. clothes, comb, brush, toothbrush, toothpaste, soap, washcloth, aspirins, knife, pencil, pen, pad, a book about slavery; 4. the past/the present; 5. nearly two months; 6. her cousin; 7. she could disappear from a moving car or take someone back with her; 8. hit her/the police; 9. books about slavery

Quiz 3 (answers will vary): 1. beaten up by Isaac; 2. didn't kill; 3. Alice and Isaac; 4. belonged to the judge; 5. Kevin had left; 6. to escape; 7. white strangers; 8. she will become a slave; 9. loves; 10. Jake/Carrie; 11. north; 12. Margaret had gone to Baltimore; 13. jumping over a broom/never legal; 14. fair; 15. had gone first to Philadelphia/talking about going to Maine; 16. she had twins; 17. Nigel had run away/Luke had been sold; 18. made Dana burn the book; 19. promised to mail the letter; 20. were captured; 21. didn't like talking about escaping; 22. Rufus bought Alice

Vocabulary

Exercise 1: 1. b; 2. a; 3. a; 4. b; 5. b; 6. c; 7. a; 8. b; 9. a; 10. b

Summarizing

Exercise 1: 1. 132; 2. 213; 3. 312; 4. 123; 5. 132; 6. 321; 7. 213

Response Journals

Exercise 1: Passage 1: S; R; R; Passage 2: R; S; S

Topics for Discussion

Exercise 1. Mind maps (answers will vary): Kevin: loves her; knows she travels to the past; knows that Rufus is her ancestor; knows that she is a writer; they met at work; their families don't approve of the marriage

Rufus: likes her; knows she comes from 1976; likes it when she reads to him; knows she saves his life; knows she is not a slave; wants her to stay with him; doesn't know why she saves him

Tom: doesn't trust Dana; thinks she can do magic; thinks Kevin is her owner; doesn't know where she goes when she disappears; thinks she's from New York

Margaret: is jealous of Dana; doesn't want Dana to read to Rufus; doesn't like it when Dana sleeps in Kevin's room; thinks she is a slave; knows that she is well educated

Exercise 2. Venn diagram: Rufus: He relies on Dana to save his life; He met Dana when he was a boy. Both: He thinks Dana is smart; He knows that Dana travels through time; He knows that Dana can write; He likes to spend time with Dana; Some members of his family don't like Dana. Kevin: He loves Dana; He knows that Rufus is Dana's ancestor.

Composition

Exercise 1: Sarah. Sample details are: the writer is black, doesn't like talking about escaping or reading books, mentioned the cookhouse and how she taught Dana to cook, etc.

Beyond the Novel

Exercise 1: 1. a; 2. b; 3. a; 4. c; 5. b; 6. c; 7. c; 8. b; 9. a; 10. b

Options

Activity 1: horizontal: Miss Hannah; Carrie; Kevin, Tom, Luke, Mr. Jennings, vertical: Margaret; Dana; Rufus; Nigel; Sarah; Buz

Unit Four

Test Yourself

Quiz 1 (answers will vary): 1. the dogs that bit Alice; 2. had been sold; 3. that he had mailed her letter; 4. Isaac's ears; 5. Rufus didn't want him to be sold; 6. Dana and Alice cooked while Sarah delivered; 7. she was a slave; 8. son/him/Jude; 9. because Tom was one slave richer; 10. that Dana had written; 11. to go to him; 12. to go to Rufus rather than run away

Quiz 2: 1. North; 2. Rufus; 3. midnight; 4. hours; 5. thrown over Rufus's horse; 6. Tom Weylin; 7. wouldn't; 8. was beaten by Alice, Tess, and Carrie; 9. Tom; 10. Tess; 11. leave right away; 12. stay

Quiz 3: 1. e; 2. a; 3. i; 4. g; 5. c; 6. j; 7. b; 8. d; 9. f; 10. h

Vocabulary

Exercise 1: inform; informative; weary; weariness; gently; gentleness; patiently; patience; comfortably; comfort; comfort; importance; importantly; silent; silently; continuation; continuous/continual; continuously/continually; angrily; anger; anger; bitter; bitterness; relaxation; curiously; curiosity; differ; different; differently; hunger; hungrily

Summarizing

Exercise 1: 1. 132; 2. 312; 3. 321; 4. 312; 5. 213

Topics for Discussion

Exercise 1: 1807 e; 1811 b; 1815 d; 1819 a; 1824 c. How old was Rufus when he tried to burn down the house? 8; almost drowned in a river? 4; fell out of a tree and broke his leg? 12; got in a fight with Isaac? 17

Exercise 2. Venn diagram: Kevin and Dana: She loves him; They are married; He is 12 years older than she is; They met at work. Both couples: He loves her; They are an interracial couple. Rufus and Alice: She was married to someone else; They are about the same age; They knew each other when they were children.

Composition

Exercise 2: Tom

Beyond the Novel

Exercise 1: 1. F.D., H.T., S.T.; 2. F.D., H.T.; 3. H.T.; 4. F.D., H.T.; 5. S.T.; 6. H.T.; 7. S.T.; 8. F.D., S.T.; 9. F.D., S.T.; 10. F.D., S.T.; 11. F.D., H.T., S.T.; 12. F.D.; 13. F.D., H.T., S.T.; 14. F.D.; 15. F.D.

Exercise 2: 1. 231; 2. 231; 3. 231

Options

Activity 1: Margaret; baby; son; Nigel; Kevin; Tom; Carrie; mother; Dana; Carrie; Sarah; Tom; Rufus. The circled letters spell: abolitionists.

Unit Five

Test Yourself
Quiz 1: 1. a, b, d; 2. b, c; 3. a, b, d; 4. b, d; 5. a, b, d
Quiz 2: 1. F; 2. T; 3. T; 4. F; 5. T; 6. F; 7. F; 8. T; 9. T; 10. T; 11. T; 12. F; 13. F; 14. T; 15. T; 16. F; 17. F; 18. T
Quiz 3 (answers will vary): 1. three; 2. they had fevers and the doctor bled and purged them; 3. she couldn't save Tom when he died; 4. work in the field; 5. cut stalks; 6. whipped her; 7. passed out; 8. get Dana; 9. not to leave; 10. she'd tried to save Tom's life; 11. he needed to punish someone; 12. Dana to take care of her; 13. opium (laudanum); 14. Hagar
Quiz 4 (answers will vary): 1. She was thin, pale, weak, kind, sweet. 2. She wanted Dana to read the Bible to her, do her laundry, clean her room. 3. Dana learned how to sew, how to tell lies, how to listen silently. 4. Dana liked working for Margaret because the work was easy, her back healed, Margaret never threatened her or tried to have her whipped. 5. A coffle looked like two dozen slaves chained two by two with handcuffs and iron collars. White men rode before and after them. 6. Carrie told Dana that if Rufus dies, all the slaves will be sold and that Dana is black no matter what the others say about her.

Vocabulary
Exercise 1: 1. confused; 2. angry; 3. unconscious; 4. help; 5. suffering; 6. died; 7. punished; 8. threatened; 9. addicted; 10. kinder
Exercise 2: 1. a; 2. b; 3. a; 4. a; 5. b

Summarizing
Exercise 1 (answers will vary): Dana is called again to Rufus and finds herself in the middle of a downpour. At first she doesn't see Rufus, but then she sees that he is face down in a puddle. She drags him away from the puddle and realizes that he is either sick or drunk. She can't carry him to the house, so she goes to get Nigel. Nigel is surprised to see her. After she and Nigel get Rufus into the house, they meet Tom. Tom tells Dana to change her clothes and come to talk to him in the library. In the library, Tom tells Dana that she's been away for six years, and he can't understand why she still has the scab on her face from where he kicked her. They argue, and Dana notices that Tom seems pale and weak. Tom tells Dana that she has to take care of Rufus.
Exercise 2: 1. to, him; 2. to, her; 3. to, him; 4. Dana, to, to, to; 5. Dana, to, to, she; 6. Dana, to; 7. to, him; 8. to, her, to; 9. to, her; 10. Dana, to, her, to

Topics for Discussion
Exercise 1 (answers will vary): 1. Altadena (It is in California, but the other two places are in Maryland.); 2. Tom (He has died, but Rufus and Kevin are alive.) OR Kevin (He is from the twentieth century, and the others are from the nineteenth century.); 3. Nigel (He wasn't sold, but the others were.); 4. the library (Slaves weren't allowed to go there, but they went to the other two places.); 5. Dana (She is not a slave, but the other two are.)
Exercise 2: 1. Tom; 2. Sarah; 3. Kevin; 4. Margaret; 5. Isaac

Exercise 4 (answers will vary): in the kitchen: microwave, food processor; in the office: computer, Internet/e-mail, fax machine, telephone answering machine; in the living room: CD player, VCR; in the news (various answers); in the sky: space shuttle

Beyond the Novel

Exercise 1: 1. D.V., N.T; 2. J.B.; 3. D.V., N.T.; 4. D.V.; 5. N.T.; 6. D.V., N.T.; 7. J.B.; 8. D.V., N.T.; 9. J.B.; 10. D.V., N.T., J.B.

Exercise 2 (answers will vary): 1767, Denmark Vesey was born; May 9, 1800, John Brown was born; October 2, 1800, Nat Turner was born; 1822, Denmark Vesey planned his revolt and was hanged; 1831, Nat Turner planned his revolt and was hanged; 1859, John Brown led his attack on the arsenal in Harpers Ferry and was hanged.

Options

Activity 1: 1. white; 2. Jude; 3. Kevin; 4. California; 5. Nigel; 6. sick; 7. Charleston; 8. cookhouse; 9. dress; 10. Harriet Tubman; 11. writer; 12. Rufus; 13. nineteenth century; 14. river on the other side; 15. Charleston

Unit Six

Test Yourself

Quiz 1: 1. dengue fever; 2. be sold; 3. help him with business matters; 4. husked the corn; 5. dance with him; 6. angry; 7. read and write; 8. free; 9. like; 10. laudanum; 11. free; 12. teach; 13. teach; 14. sold; 15. cut her wrists

Quiz 2 (answers will vary): 1. so that she would think she was going to die and go home; 2. Kevin's doctor friend, Louis George; 3. killing him or letting him die; 4. all the slaves will be sold; she might need some power that she taps in him to come home; 5. because Alice killed herself; Rufus is considering suicide; 6. in the barn; 7. Alice thought Rufus had sold her children; 8. to the library to get his gun; 9. had sent them to Baltimore to teach Alice a lesson after she ran away; 10. certificates of freedom for the children; 11. certificates of freedom; 12. that she would not save him; 13. to the attic; 14 a knife; 15. on her arm; 16. Nigel; 17. it was stuck in the wall; 18. to Maryland; 19. burned the house; 20. they were sold

Quiz 3 (answers will vary): Page 228: Rufus tells Dana and Alice that he considers them to be two halves of one woman. Page 229: Dana tells Alice that they do look alike, and Alice says that they are two parts of the same woman to Rufus. Page 229: Dana tells how the slaves had mixed feelings toward Rufus. Page 230: Dana and Rufus are talking about Dana finding a man, and Rufus shows that he is jealous and wants Dana for himself. Page 233: Alice shows that she is determined to run away and find freedom for herself and her children. Page 234: After the birth of Hagar, Dana sees Alice smile at Rufus. She thinks Alice is beginning to like Rufus. Page 234: This shows that Rufus respects Alice's choice of the name even though he thinks it is ugly. Alice chose it from the Bible. Dana thinks it is the most beautiful name she has ever heard because Hagar will be her ancestor and now she doesn't have to keep Rufus safe anymore. Page 235: Alice says that Rufus won't free her or her children. He always wants more. People claim that she really likes Rufus, and she wants to run away before she really does begin to like him. Page 242: Kevin thinks that Dana should kill Rufus now that Hagar is born. Page 243: Dana lost her independence just when the United States was celebrating 200 years of independence. (July 4 is Independence Day; July 4, 1976, was the Bicentennial.)

Vocabulary

Exercise 1: 1. a. silently; b. silent; c. silence; 2. a. persuade; b. persuasive; c. persuasion; 3. a. patient; b. patiently; c. patience; 4. a. curiosity; b. curious; c. curiously; 5. a. angrily; b. angry; c. anger; 6. a. endanger; b. dangerous; c. dangers; 7. a. cautiously; b. caution; c. cautious; 8. a. innocent; b. innocence; c. innocently; 9. a. desperately; b. desperation; c. desperate; 10. a. differ; b. differences; c. different

Summarizing

Exercise 1 (answers will vary): Dana started to teach some of the slave children to read and write. Some of Rufus's neighbors found out, and they thought it was dangerous to teach slaves. One day, a slave named Sam stopped Dana outside the cookhouse. He was the slave who had asked her to dance at the Christmas party. Sam wanted Dana to teach his brother and sister how to read and write. Dana told him not to talk to her again, to talk to Sarah instead. A few days later, Rufus sold Sam. Dana was angry. She cut her wrists and traveled back to the present.

Exercise 2: 1. that would would her; 2. that he her him him; 3. that she her that hit her she hit; 4. that was her; 5. that wanted her; 6. that had come her; 7. that didn't him she had her; 8. that she didn't she was she did found him; 9. that she had sold her she that; 10. that was that was she could

Topics for Discussion

Exercise 1. Venn diagram: Alice: She was born free; Her husband was sold; She wanted her children to learn to read; She tried to run away. Both: She was a slave; She was married to a slave; She lost her husband; She had children who were fathered by a white man; She believed that her children were sold; She had the opportunity to kill her master; Her master promised freedom to her or her children. Sarah: She was born a slave; Her husband was killed in an accident; She was afraid of education; She didn't like to think about running away.

Beyond the Novel

Exercise 1: Check these statements: Dana attended a segregated kindergarten class . . . ; When Dana was two, her father was not permitted to vote . . . ; As a young teenager, Dana attended the March on Washington . . . ; Dana saw riots in Los Angeles . . . ;
Exercise 2: 1. 123; 2. 231; 3. 132; 4. 213

Options

Activity 1: 1. j; 2. n; 3. o; 4. q; 5. u; 6. s; 7. f; 8. t; 9. h; 10. v; 11. k; 12. e; 13. p; 14. l; 15. r; 16. b; 17. m; 18. a; 19. g; 20. o; 21. d; 22. i

Printed and bound by CPI Group (UK) Ltd, Croydon, CR0 4YY

09/06/2025

14685680-0001